Automatic Recruiting System

The Easy Way to Make a Huge Fortune from the Comfort of Your Home!

T.J. Rohleder

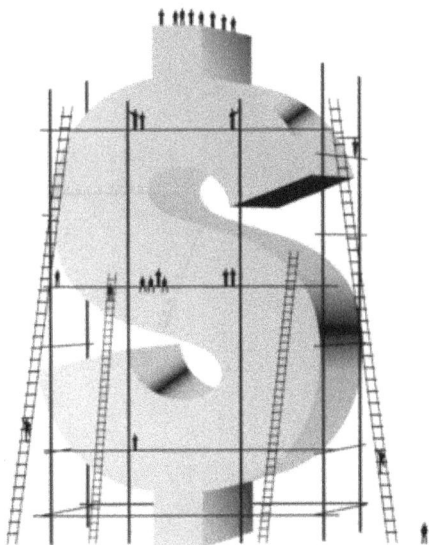

You can have anything
in life you want,
if you'll only help
enough other people
get what they want.

– Zig Ziglar

*Thank you Al Branca for
making all of this possible!*

Bethesda Discount Prescriptions
103 South Elm Street
Goessel, Kansas 67053

FIRST EDITION

ISBN 1-933356-75-8

TABLE OF CONTENTS

FORWARD

By Russ von Hoelscher

A Business in a Book!

Do you sincerely want to make a lot of money part time?

To always have the money you want and need, no matter what happens?

If your answer is a positive "YES!", then reading this book is one of the smartest things you'll ever do. Author T.J. Rohleder will show you how easy it is to make money with the same 3 steps that brought him millions of dollars. These simple steps can give you all the money and freedom you need. ABSOLUTELY ANYONE CAN DO IT, regardless of age, experience, or education. T.J. and his staff can even do most of these 3 steps for you, if you want.

My name is Russ von Hoelscher. I am a marketing consultant who first taught these methods to T.J. and his wife Eileen many years ago. Thanks to my help, support and guidance the Rohleder's became millionaires in a few short years.

Now T.J. has discovered the most amazing way to make even more money by helping a small group of others profit with these 3 steps. But don't worry. You don't need his help to make money. You can do this entirely on your own, if you wish.

Section One of this book is the definitive guide on the pros and cons of the Network or Affiliate Marketing business. Then in Section Two, you'll discover how to make money in any of these types of opportunities, without the headaches and hassles that most people who are in this business are forced to go through.

Millions of people desperately want and need to make more money. Most of them have been exposed to a Network or Affiliate Marketing opportunity. They like some of the benefits of this business, such as the low start-up cost, residual income, being part of a team, and making money by helping others. But they hate the traditional recruiting methods that force them to bother their friends and family.

But You Won't Have These Problems!

Because the methods T.J. will give you in Section Two and the amazing opportunity he will tell you about in Section Three shows you how to get all the benefits this business has to offer, without the headaches and hassles. This separates you from

99% of everyone else and makes the best people want to join your team.

The Greek shipping billionaire Aristotle Onassis once said "the secret to business is to know something none of your competitors knows." That one idea brought him billions of dollars. Now his secret can make you massive sums of money! Here's how: the system T.J. will be telling you about is built around a marketing method known as "Direct Response Marketing." This is something most Network Marketers and the companies they promote know nothing about. This form of marketing generates billions of dollars every year. It eliminates the need for personal selling. The only people you talk with are those who are already 100% pre-sold and ready to join. This gives you a genuine unfair advantage over all the other network marketers.

With my help, T.J. and his wife became

multi-millionaires in a few short years thanks to the power of Direct Response Marketing. Now T.J. has taken the best of the best of all of the powerful secrets he's used to generate millions of dollars and built them into this powerful time-tested system. With these methods, it doesn't matter where you live. His company is headquartered in a small town in the middle of Kansas and yet he has used these marketing methods to do business with over one million people. Think about that. Then consider the power this can give you!

YOU CAN TRUST T.J. ROHLEDER.

T.J. struggled financially for many years. He knew there were huge numbers of other people who were also suffering. All these people needed was the right opportunity and they could make huge sums of money. And he was right! He and Eileen started in September of 1988 with a few hundred dollars. They started making money right away, because they began their business with a really great idea. I met them six months later. I saw their first ad and wrote to tell them how much I liked what they were doing. I told them I was confident I could help them make even more money.

So the Rohleder's hired me. We spent some time on the phone and I gave them a few of my greatest secrets. Then they paid me $2,500 to fly to Kansas and spend a couple days sharing even more of my closely guarded get-rich secrets. I ended up giving them dozens of my most proven strategies that they could put to immediate use. And the marketing secrets I gave them (many of which are in this book) worked like magic! Within 9 months, they were bringing in total sales of almost $100,000 a week. I've helped them bring in sales of tens of millions of dollars since then.

That's how I know that getting personal help

and having a private friendship with other business builders and millionaires can help you make all the money you want, need and truly deserve. And now, T.J. will share some of these greatest secrets with you. These are some of the best secrets I first gave to him, mixed with many of the greatest ideas he discovered on his own. As you'll see, this lets you make money part time with the best secrets that have brought him many millions of dollars. All this can help you…

Become One of The Top Distributors in Any Network or Affiliate Marketing Company.

Here's the premise behind this extremely comprehensive book: Millions of people would love to get paid the huge residual incomes that these types of opportunities provide, BUT…

✔   They don't want to sell…

✔   They don't want to bother their friends

and family...

✔   They hate going to opportunity meetings and pep rallies.

If only these people could make huge sums of residual income without these headaches and hassles, wouldn't that be great?

Well now they can! Because thanks to the little-known methods and strategies T.J. will give you in this book, you'll be helping them do it. This 3-step Automatic Recruiting System gives you the power to: (A) become a top distributor in any company or (B) work directly with Mr. Rohleder and his staff and let them do their best to help you make huge sums of money in the Affiliate Opportunity he will tell you about in Section Three.

I have thoroughly looked over the

opportunity you'll read about in the final Section of this book and I'm very excited about it! I immediately became an Affiliate, because it's so much different and better than most of the other opportunities I've seen over the last 40 years. And if you choose to join this opportunity, too, then T.J. and his staff will be using the methods you'll read about in this book to do most of the work for you! If that happens, he will be…

YOUR FRIEND IN THE BUSINESS.

With that in mind, remember this: The main character trait that separates the winners from the losers are the friends you keep and the people you know. And that's good news for you, because when you go through this book and follow the simple instructions at the end of Section Three, you'll have powerful friends in the business who will help you every step of the way.

This is so important to your ultimate success

– I must say it again...

It's Not Always WHAT You Know.
It's WHO You Know and WHO
You're Getting Your Personal Help
from That Can Help You Get Rich.

Do you really want financial freedom? Then start by associating with others who are already rich. This is a true wealth secret that brought T.J. and his wife millions of dollars and can change your life!

Here's the God's-Honest Truth: T.J. and Eileen would not be millionaires today if it wasn't for the help I gave them in the beginning (or another expert like myself). I became their friend in the business. I took them by the hand and showed them the way to get rich. I was the friend who told them exactly what to do and how to do it. I guided them. I revealed the secrets behind the 3 simple steps that T.J will give you in this book. These secrets took me over 20 years to discover! I told them what to do, and, even more importantly, what not to do. I became their close friend and 'coach' in the business. That made all the difference in the world. It can make all the difference for you, too.

You need successful friends and mentors who can help you the same way I helped the Rohleder's. Why? Because…

You Will Never Make a
Lot of Money By Yourself.

You need the help of successful people who started with very little and have gone on to making huge sums of money. You need friends who have already done it. These are the only people who can truly help you make money. You don't need your brother-in-law, or your neighbor.

You need someone who's done it themselves. And you need friends who believe in you when nobody else does.

Plus, you need experts like T.J. and his hand-picked staff to call on when you need help. You need a super successful team of winners who will show you how to make the largest sum of money in the fastest time. You need people who truly care about you and your success. You need people who want to do all they can to help you make money because they make money for doing all they can to make you money. You need all the rich friends you can find who are ready, willing and able to include you in on their very best money-making projects. This is what you'll receive when you go through this book and follow the simple instructions at the end.

THE DEMAND FOR THIS BOOK IS ENORMOUS!

Tens of millions of people have been

exposed to Network Marketing. Some of those people have been involved in one or two of these types of opportunities. Many others have watched their friends and family members get involved in these opportunities, get their hopes up, and then fail. All of this has led to a huge and growing number of folks who have a strong dislike for the Network and Affiliate Marketing industry. But when these people see that you have a system that allows them to attract other distributors with no personal selling and then quickly and easily help them do the same, they will take notice.

Because in the end what these people really hate is not Network or Affiliate Marketing – it's the traditional recruiting methods that are being promoted by these companies. They know there's a tremendous amount of money to be made in this business. They've heard the stories of others who started with virtually nothing and have gone on to make high six and even seven-figure annual incomes. The Automatic Recruiting System T.J. will teach you in this book is designed to attract these people by showing them how they can build a substantial income in any company without the headaches and hassles of traditional methods. Once they see that, they'll join your team and become loyal distributors who can make you money for years.

So with all this said, go on to the Introduction and then the three Sections of this book. Let T.J. Rohleder reveal these secrets to you and then tell you about the revolutionary home based business opportunity he has built his automated system for. You'll see: the opportunity he has for you is not traditional Network Marketing. However, it does pay on several levels. And best of all, it gives you (and the people that T.J. and his staff can sign up under you) an exciting new way to make money by helping others! Please go through this book for all of the details. Then fill out the last page and let T.J. help you get started at once.

Russ von Hoelscher,
Hoelscher Marketing Group
El Cajon, California
(619) 588-2155

INTRODUCTION

Hi, my name is T.J. Rohleder. Since 1988, I've made millions from a small town in the middle of Kansas, thanks to an unusual marketing method I'll tell you about.

For the last few years, my business partners and I have been combining our powerful marketing secrets with Network Marketing to earn big commissions without any personal selling! And now I want to share these secrets and strategies with as many people like you who love the idea of making money in Network Marketing but hate all of the headaches and hassles you must go through to build your own sales organization.

I'm hoping you may want to make money

with me.

My research has led to a very special opportunity we call the "EASY PASSIVE INCOME SYSTEM." This is not a traditional Network Marketing Program, but it does pay on several levels. As you'll see, this is designed to let you get started dirt-cheap and pocket up to thousands of dollars a month in no time flat! I am looking for people who want to join us and cash-in with our automated System that does the selling for you. I hope that by giving you the secrets behind my Automatic Recruiting System, you may be willing to take a serious look at this opportunity and consider making money with me.

But don't worry. Because you do NOT have to join my team to profit with these little-known methods. You can use them to make money in any Network Marketing company with NO personal selling.

So let's begin. For starters, have you ever wondered why many Network Marketers struggle to make money, while others make $100,000 a year or much more?

The answer is simple: These professionals are always able to make huge sums of money without the problems that others must go through, because they've discovered a proven way to sign up thousands of people into their team. You are about to discover how to do this, too, and be in position to get paid a huge six figure income!

Wait – did I just say you could earn $100,000 a year or more?

YES! In fact, the top people in this industry make over that much every month!

JUST LOOK: Here's what the top-10

AUTOMATIC RECRUITING SYSTEM

Network Marketers earn:

NAME / COMPANY / ESTIMATED MONTHLY INCOME

Dexter and Birdie Yager / Amway / $1.3 million

Juha Parhiala / OneCoin / $1 million

Shane Morand / Organo Gold / $1 million

Rolf Kipp / Forever Living Products / $780,000

Brian McClure / Ambit Energy / $700,000

Kim Hui / Jeunesse Global / $550,000

Steinkeller Brothers / OneCoin / $550,000

Barry Chi and Holly Chen / Amway / $500,000

Angela Liew and Ryan Ho / Nu Skin Enterprises / $500,000

Foo Howe Kean and Jenny Ko / Amway / $400,000

This list came from BusinessForHome.org.
This is the premier source for the global Network

Marketing industry. (They have a database of the top 8,000+ earners in Network Marketing, updated every 30 minutes in real time. So this list will be outdated by the time you read it. I'm reprinting it here so you can see the kind of money the top performers are making.) Anyway, as you'll come to understand, many these top heavy-hitters who are making $400,000 to $1,300,000 a month are doing it because they've mastered the main secret of.

A Powerful Marketing System.

This could pay you more money than most Doctors make, because...

1. It can bring you hundreds or even thousands of the most dedicated, loyal, committed and hardest working distributors. You will attract these winners and make them eager to sign up under you.

2.   Your distributors can also use it to make big money from the efforts of others.

Listen, most network marketers don't make any money to speak of. But once you see how my own proven multi-million dollar system works – you can cash-in with your own proven Marketing System that's designed to make you and your future distributors huge sums of easy money.

Best of all, in a few short minutes from now you can register to get the secrets behind my complete and proven system that's designed to.

Quickly Make You Big Money Without
Bothering Your Friends and Family
or Having to Talk with Anyone!

My millionaire-making experts and I have discovered the ultimate secrets that have the power to make you super rich. The few who know the secrets that have gone into our system are making

GIANT sums of money. Most will never share these secrets of success with you. But we will!

As you'll see, we have stumbled onto the greatest secrets that let you make huge sums of money in Network Marketing. This lets you cash-in without any personal selling or old-fashioned recruiting methods that force you to try to sign up all of your friends and family and bother everyone you know.

Best of all.

You'll make your fortune by doing the opposite of what everyone else is doing.

Here are the basics: Most people think they have to learn how to be a master salesperson or recruiter to make a ton of money in Network Marketing. They believe the only way to make a lot of money is to call people up approach strangers and face all kinds of personal rejection.

This is the kind of nonsense that most Network Marketing "experts" tell you to do.

Yuck! Who wants to sell stuff face-to-face for a living? Not me. I'm sure you don't either. Too much damn rejection.

More on this later.

For now, consider these 2 Facts:

FACT #1:

The world is filled with millions of people who have been taught that bothering their friends and family and approaching everyone they know is the "only way" to make money in Network Marketing.

These people have experienced nothing but false promises and broken dreams.

FACT #2:

However, there are also many, many Network Marketing Millionaires. And some of these people are making money without the headaches and hassles of personal selling and traditional recruiting methods. We want to show you how to join this exclusive group.

These people are living on easy street. They generate commissions of $10,000... $30,000... and even $50,000 a month or more. They are the top 1% of the money-makers. And you can be one of them!

These people are living the American Dream because they found a legitimate Network Marketing opportunity and are using an Marketing System that lets them make money without the hassles that other Distributors go through.

And now you can join them! Believe me, you can easily do this when you learn the secrets I will share you.

Here's a BIG PART of the secret: the way to create a System that lets you get rich in Network Marketing without any personal selling is by mixing it with the little-known marketing method that has made me and my friends millions of dollars, called.

"DIRECT RESPONSE."

This time-tested marketing method gives you the power to make up to tens or even hundreds of thousands of dollars a year in Network Marketing with zero rejection.

Our proven 3-Step System lets you:

A.   Reach up to thousands of people who are perfect for your Network Marketing opportunity and quickly get rid of the ones who end up wasting your time.

B.   Attract the very best people who want to join your opportunity.

C.   Avoid talking to anyone. If you do talk with anyone (your choice) it will only be the people who are most serious, already pre-sold and ready to make you big money.

With my proven Automatic Recruiting System, you can make huge sums of money in ANY Network Marketing opportunity without the headaches and hassles of traditional recruiting methods. Or you can get involved with me and make money with my complete System that I'll give you for free.

Does all this sound too good to be true?

Well it's not! And if you'll keep an open mind and get the secrets behind our proven 3-Step System, you'll be in for quite a surprise! How big? Well, the first time I used these methods in a Network Marketing program, I got paid.

$234,795 in 9 weeks.

That's right –these same no-rejection methods made me almost a quarter of a million dollars in 9 weeks.

How's that for proof?

The only reason I tell you about my $234,795 in 9 weeks is to prove that my unique Automatic Recruiting System works like magic!

All of this money was made without me having to talk with a single person!

Please don't think I'm trying to show off. I'm not. However, I am bragging about the marketing secrets that have made my friends and I millions of dollars.

These secrets are making many other lucky people super rich.

We're doing it with no personal selling. And now, you can cash in with of our secrets!

The Direct Response Marketing methods that have gone into my Automatic Recruiting System generate hundreds of billions of dollars a year. However, this is still a highly misunderstood form of marketing, because it has many variables that are hidden from the novice. These are secrets that most insiders keep to themselves.

But now you can get our time-tested secrets that we have boiled down into a simple 3-step system you can use to get rich in any Network Marketing program!

Here's what it's all about: Two of my good friends and I have spent the last seven years compiling our greatest secrets that have made us millions. Now we have reduced the best-of-the-best of all of these secrets into a simple 3-step system that you can use to make huge sums of money in any Network Marketing opportunity. This amazing system has the power to make you massive sums of money!

The few who know these secrets are fighting to keep them quiet. But we're blowing the lid off these little know tips, tricks and strategies! They're all yours in this complete turn-key system that you can receive for free.

You'll discover how:

- Step #1 makes people stand in line and practically beg you to let them join your team.

- Step #2 makes you massive money in lightning speed!

- Step #2 finds the best people who will make you big money for many years.
- Step #3 gives you 100% FREE ADVERTISING that recruits large numbers of people.

These are secrets you won't get anywhere else until now!

More on all this later. For now, just know.

This book is being written for the tens of millions of people who love and hate Network Marketing.

If you are part of the later group – I understand completely. I've been there, too. But even if you have had some bad experiences with Network Marketing the fact that you are reading this right now tells me that you haven't given up on Network Marketing completely. You are (hopefully) still open and receptive to some of the main ideas I will be sharing with you. So – you see – as bad as most Network Marketing opportunities are there is no way you can deny the simple fact that many average people are super rich right now because they joined a Network Marketing Program. Now these people are walking to their mailbox every week or month and pulling out huge checks for more money then most doctors or lawyers ever dream of making!!

I am living proof that it is very possible to make many tens of thousands of dollars a month in Network Marketing. In fact, I have brought in over $100,000 a year in many different Network Marketing companies. I'm not telling you this to brag. But I only bring up my own success for two reasons: # 1: I am living proof that it's possible to make tens of thousands of dollars a month in Network Marketing. #2: I have earned these GIANT sums of monthly income without any of the headaches and hassles of traditional recruiting methods.

Let me take a moment to tell you about both of these items.

1.   When it comes to making money – everyone has an opinion. But you must only listen to people who have made a lot of money. Ignore everything else. Only someone who has made a lot of money can show you how to do it, too.

Because of this – I had to start this book by telling you that I have made hundreds of thousands of dollars in Network Marketing. In fact, I have made over $100,000 a year in many different Network Marketing companies, so I do speak with some real authority. But many people have made way more then I have. In fact, many average people have made millions in Network Marketing – and that's what makes the next item on my list even more exciting.

2.   All of the money I have made in

Network Marketing came to me without any of the headaches and hassles most distributors are forced to go through. In fact, I made most of this money without talking to a single person and NEVER personally selling anything to anybody!

Yes, item #2 on my list of reasons I'm telling you about my success is the most important. You see – many people have and are making a fortune in Network Marketing right now – but these people are forced to through a tremendous amount of headaches and hassles to earn their wealth:

- ✔ They must learn how to become master salespeople and dynamic public speakers.

- ✔ They spend hours on the phone every day.

✔ They travel from city to city and live out of a suitcase.

✔ Etc. Etc.

As you will see the #1 reason why traditional Network Marketing sucks is because of all the personal selling and personal promotional work you have to do to recruit new distributors into your down line and then somehow get them to do the same thing. If you have ever tried to do this, you know how miserable it can be. The fact that most Network Marketing companies do not tell you that you must become a charismatic salesperson – dynamic public speaker – and fearless leader and sales person of other people in order to get rich is also one of the main reasons Network Marketing really does suck!

But I am living proof that you really can make enormous sums of money in Network Marketing without all of these headaches and hassles.

In fact, at the time I am writing this to you, I am bringing well over $100,000 a year in just one of the opportunities that I'll help you cash in with. Best of all, I'm making this money – without doing hardly anything. Again, I do not say this to brag. I hate people who try to be big shots and boast about all the money they're making – I'm sure you can't stand these types of people either. No, the only reason I tell you about the money I have and am now making in Network Marketing is because I have discovered the true secret to getting rich in Network Marketing without any of the headaches and hassles that most Distributors are going through right now. Best of all, my secrets of how you can make a fortune in Network Marketing with zero personal selling and without even talking to a single person (unless you want to) are in this small book!

Yes, this book gives you the basic secrets,

that a small group of lucky people like myself have discovered, to getting rich in Network Marketing without any personal selling! This is definitely not too good to be true! Right now as you are reading this – there are many people who are using the basic secrets I'll be giving you to make huge sums of money without any of the headaches and hassles most distributors make on a daily basis. Best of all, now you can be next! Just go through this small book from cover to cover – and follow the simple instructions at the end. And with that in mind.

Here's what you're about to discover in this book:

- I'll cover some of the main problems that almost all Network Marketing distributors are forced to go through on a daily basis. You will read this section and fully understand why

Network Marketing does not work for most people.

- I will reveal the secret that has let me and a small group of other lucky people make a fortune in Network Marketing with zero personal selling and without any of the headaches and hassles most distributors are going through.

- You will learn a little about a very special opportunity we call: "EASY PASSIVE INCOME SYSTEM." This lets you cash in with the wealth making secrets you'll discover in this book!

I believe this very special opportunity is the ultimate way to get rich in Network Marketing without any personal selling! As you'll see when you read this third and final section – I have discovered and developed a powerful new opportunity that completely eliminates the biggest problems almost all Network Marketing companies have in common. Best of all – you can cash in with me and use my simple system that is designed to make you BIG MONEY in as little as 10 minutes a day!

SECTION ONE

A Crash Course on the Good, the Bad and the Ugly Side of the Network Marketing Industry.

This Section tells you about some of the main problems that almost all Network Marketing distributors are forced to go through on a daily basis. Study this section to fully understand why most people never make any significant sum of money in Network Marketing.

<u>CHAPTER ONE</u>

The Magic Power of Residual Income!

And Why You Should LOVE So Many Things About Network Marketing.

Do you love Network Marketing?

Or do you hate it?

Well, if you're like me, it's a little of both.

I'll tell you all the reasons I HATE IT in the

next Chapter. And these are things you should think very deeply about. Because as you'll see in this book, this business can be make you financially set for life, but only after you wake up to certain "UGLY TRUTHS" about it and learn to make money in spite of them.

But I want to start with THE GOOD THINGS! So in this Chapter we'll talk about the main reasons why you should LOVE this business. The main thing is:

Residual Income!

All Network Marketing opportunities let you tap into the power of residual income. Because this powerful wealth-making method can make you a millionaire in no time flat, it's by far the #1 secret behind the world's richest people!

So what is residual income, and why is it so

powerful? Simply put, residual income is all the money you can make without exerting any of your own time and effort which, of course, is directly the opposite of how most people get paid – by the hour – and since there are only 168 hours in a week, the amount of money they can make is always limited. But the world's richest people use the power of residual income to make all their money because they're getting paid on many other elements, besides their time and effort.

In other words, the amount of money they make has little to nothing to do with the number of hours they work! Residual income is the reason why the richest people in the world can play around on the golf course every day and still make BIG money – or they can take exotic vacations while the money keeps flowing in – or, even better, they can take a month or two off, while their income just keeps getting bigger and bigger!

They can even retire and do absolutely nothing

– while the money keeps coming in like clockwork!

Imagine what your life would be like if you could take off for a month or two and still keep getting huge sums of money! Think about how things could be for you if you could make money while shopping, sleeping, or spending quality time with family and friends. How would your life change if the amount of money you made had absolutely nothing to do with the number of hours you put in? Well, one thing for sure is that you'd end up with an awful lot of joy and happiness!

And this is what residual income can do for you! With this type of income, the amount of money you make has nothing to do with how much time and work you exert! For the first time in your life you'll be free to do whatever you want! You can shop, sleep, or vacation, and still get paid! You can enjoy your life while relaxing, and the money will keep flowing in!

This may sound like a dream, but it's not!

Millions of people all over the world have discussed how to tap into the power of residual income! These people do not have to worry about where their next dollar is going to come from – instead, they simply relax and enjoy life, knowing that they are financially secure, no matter what!

And, here's the kicker: Some of these lucky people are Network Marketing distributors!

Yes, Network Marketing gives you the opportunity to make money with residual income! I know – it sounds simple enough – just build a huge down-line of distributors, then sit back, relax, and get paid from their efforts! And all you have to do is find 5 people who find 5 people who find 5 more people, etc., and so forth. Soon the numbers will multiply, and you'll have thousands of people in your group. Now, how difficult can that be? Right?

Right! It doesn't sound difficult because it isn't difficult! And after you see the possibilities, you're hooked because now you can see how you really could have thousands of people making money for you night and day – now you can almost see yourself walking to your mailbox every month and pulling out a giant check for thousands of dollars – now you're on Easy Street – now you're excited because you have discovered a better way to make money – and now, at last, you see how it's possible to sit back and let other people make money for you! And you become obsessed with the idea of residual income!

Soon you're hit with a powerful life-changing idea. You understand for the first time in your life why the rich get richer and the poor get poorer. And you know why 90% of all the people in the world – who only get paid by the hour – will never be rich. Now you comprehend one of the main things you must understand if you want to get rich: If you want to make a lot of money, you must get paid on many things, not just on the amount of time you work.

This simple idea will change your life – which is why it's the primary reason I love Network Marketing!

This important, wealth-making principle of residual income is not taught in school. In fact, most people don't even realize that getting paid by the hour is the worst way to make money. They first discover the secret of residual income at some Network Marketing Pep Rally or opportunity meeting and, once they see that working for an hourly wage is dangerous to their wealth, their lives are changed forever! And I know this to be fact because my wife, Eileen, and I are two of those people! Our lives changed completely the moment one of my friends, a coworker at the time, tried to get us to join a famous Network Marketing company.

We went over to his house at eight at night. He drew the circles for us and showed us the awesome power of getting paid from the efforts of thousands of other people. More importantly, he showed us why we would never get rich as long as we were paid an hourly wage, and he introduced us to the awesome power of residual income – and we were hooked for life! Now, when we think back to those early years, we can still vividly recall leaving his home at one o'clock in the morning, so excited that we couldn't sleep! We had caught a glimpse of what was possible for our lives. We finally realized that we could have everything in life we wanted. We saw how it was possible for us to stay where we were and build a business through the power of Network Marketing. Before that night, we had a lot of ambition, after that night, we knew that we really could make millions of dollars – and once that vision seized us, there was no turning back!

Yes, not only did that night change our lives forever, it also made us millionaires...

Let me clarify... we never got rich in Network Marketing (actually, truth be known, few do), however, we did discover the power of residual income and, with this knowledge, we learned that there are countless numbers of ways for average people – like you and me – to make a fortune with residual income. And although Network Marketing does indeed have the ability to make money with this kind of income, it's probably the worst way in the world to do it!

Fact: Out of all the countless numbers of ways there are to get rich with residual income, Network Marketing is by far the absolute worst! But then, on the other hand, if it weren't for Network Marketing, Eileen and I probably never would have heard of residual income in the first place, so it's sort of like a catch 22! And I'll bet there are millions of other people just like us, who first discovered the awesome power of getting rich from a myriad of other things besides just the number of hours we work!

So, thank goodness for Network Marketing! Even though most people will never make any significant money in it, there are plenty of millionaires out there who owe their fortunes to discovering this powerful wealth-making secret called residual income, which segues right into the second reason I love Network Marketing:

Self-Employment!

There are over 30 million self-employed people in America today, and this number is growing! These people have discovered the pure joy that comes from having their own business. In fact, many of them got their very first taste of self-employment by joining some kind of Network Marketing company!

As mentioned, Eileen and I got our start through Network Marketing, which provided us with our first taste of being our own bosses. In the early 1980s, we had zero skills or experience – but we did have a burning desire to do big things with our lives. And getting involved in all the various Network Marketing opportunities was the powerful experience that provided us with the impetus we needed to do just that, so much so, in fact, that we soon realized that we would not be millionaires today if it hadn't been for that early introduction to Network Marketing.

Certainly, there's no way to know for sure, but conceivably there could be literally millions of people just like we were back in those early days: We were not happy with our lives, we were always broke and could barely pay our bills, and we knew there had to be more out of life. After all, America was the greatest country on earth, the land of the free and home of the brave, the land of the proverbial "milk and honey." We knew there were average people out there who were making a fortune, and we wondered why we couldn't do the same. Like them, we wanted to live in a nice home, drive a good car, take lots of vacations, put our kids through school, and give money to our church and community. So when that friend I mentioned introduced us to our first Network Marketing company, we were ready!

Of course, it took about 10 years after that night before we actually did become millionaires! First, we had to go through a lot of struggle and pain. There was much to learn, and we had considerable growing up to do (especially me!). But the fact remains: Had it not been for all those crazy Network Marketing experiences, we would not be where we are today, which ties in with the third reason why I love Network Marketing:

Millions of self-employed people owe their success to Network Marketing because...

- Network Marketing makes it super easy to start your own business!

- Network Marketing helps you to realize that you really can get rich!

- Network Marketing helps you to develop certain skills you must have to make a lot of money!

- Network Marketing gives you an easy way to become friends with other entrepreneurs!

Since these areas are really relevant, let's

take a moment to discuss each a bit further...

Thanks to Network Marketing, starting your own business is super easy!

Most people have thought about starting their own business...

✔ But the price is too great...

✔ There are too many hurdles to go over to have your own company...

✔ It takes a lot of time and hard work...

✔ You have to figure out a million different things (at least!)...

✔ And there's a lot of pain and frustration.

They desperately want to be their own boss,

call their own shots, and do their "own thing."

They want everything a business can give them:

✔   More money...

✔   Freedom to do what they want...

✔   Self-esteem and a feeling of
      accomplishment...

✔   And the satisfaction that comes from
      building a solid company from scratch.

But no matter how badly they want all of
these things, the obstacles hold them back. The
forces against them are just too great, and their
doubts begin to mount: They can't give up the
safety and security of their job! They can't put
their family at risk! After all, they've worked hard
all their lives to get where they are, and they can't

risk everything to start their own company.

But Network Marketing takes away all the obstacles! All you have to do now to become self-employed is pay a small fee and become a distributor for an Network Marketing company! This is great! Now you are officially self-employed, and all it cost was less than $100! You fill out the Distributor Agreement Form, pay your small fee, and choose a company name – and that's it! And most Network Marketing companies will even print your business cards and stationery!

These companies are a blessing for millions of ambitious people because they provide us with an easy way to have our own businesses! Now our fantasy of having our own company is a reality, a dream come true!

Network Marketing shows us that it really is possible to make a lot of money!

People love to fantasize about getting rich (come on, admit it – we all do!). But do they really believe that they actually can get rich? Probably not, after all, their parents and relatives aren't rich. In fact, most, if not all, of the people they grew up with are lucky to even be able to pay their bills each month and keep a roof over their heads, so why should things be different for them?

So, if your friends and family can't show you how to get rich, who can? School? No, teachers certainly aren't rich! And there are no classes to show you how to make a lot of money. Oh, sure, most schools teach Business and Economics, but these classes are designed to help you become an executive at some company out there in Corporate America.

Bottom line: There's almost nowhere, anyplace, where you can go that teaches Entrepreneurship. So, if there's nobody, anywhere, teaching young people how to turn small sums of money into a small fortune, is it any wonder why we grow up doubting our ability to get rich? Of course not!

BUT there are places – albeit, very few – where you can go to learn how to turn your ambition into dollars. And one of those places is Network Marketing.

Network Marketing is a life-changing experience for many of us: We get involved with these companies and are surrounded with other ambitious people just like us. We hear all the stories about average people who are supposedly making $10,000 to $50,000 to even $100,000 a month, or more! And we learn the company's marketing plan and see (at least on paper!) that we really can get rich, and this opens and expands our awareness! We get a new vision and see ourselves as having all the money we want!

And this new vision makes us hungrier for wealth, which, in turn, makes us even more ambitious than before!

The exciting possibilities we discover through Network Marketing is like throwing gasoline on a fire! And once we get this new vision for ourselves, we are changed forever. Now there's no going back! We're committed, and nothing can stop us! We've caught the entrepreneurial bug, and we're hooked for life! Our desire for all of the best things in life becomes stronger, and we're more serious about getting rich than ever before!

Network Marketing helps us develop the skills we need to get rich!

Now we are Network Marketing distributors with a whole new level of ambition and commitment! Our dreams of making a lot of money are stronger than ever, and the possibilities seem endless! What started out as pure ambition has now become something far greater. We're motivated and even more serious about getting rich! And Network Marketing is where we develop the main skills we need to become millionaires...

- Positive Motivation

- People Skills

- Public Speaking

- Goal Setting

- And Salesmanship!

Network Marketing teaches us that if we want to make a lot of money we must work on ourselves first. We must let go of our old attitudes and behaviors and start setting goals to clarify what we really want. We must learn how to stay positive and motivated (these are learned skills). We must teach ourselves how to face our biggest fears and insecurities, and develop new attitudes and success-oriented behaviors!

In short, Network Marketing teaches us that for our lives to change, we must change.

One of my most influential Network Marketing sponsors used to get up in front of hundreds of distributors and shout: "If you always think the way you always thought, you'll always get what you always got!" And, it's so true!

Our success (or lack thereof) boils down to these key ingredients:

- Having big goals and a positive attitude.

- Being so determined that nothing can

stop you.

- Taking full responsibility for your own life.

- And most important: Learning how to sell!

Network Marketing teaches us the importance of selling. For the first time in our lives, we realize that nobody makes any money until something is sold! Every person in the world owes their job to salespeople. We're the ones who bring in all the money! Nobody would get a paycheck if it weren't for the work we do. We're the heroes who build the businesses that others manage!

Salesmanship is vital to the success of every business. Think about it...

No company ever went out of business because it had too many sales and profits!

Salesmanship is the one key ingredient that separates the winners from the losers in any business. Without strong sales and profits, there is no business. It's the life-giving bloodline of every company – cut it off and the business will die.

Selling is the Key Ingredient
in Network Marketing.

Everyone in Network Marketing is taught to sell the opportunity, sell the products, and sell themselves – and not necessarily in that order. More simply put, Network Marketing is nothing more than a channel of distribution to selling and getting products and services into the hands of the end consumer.

And, until we join our first Network Marketing company, most of us do not understand the vital role that selling plays in our society!

Network Marketing provides you with a

better class of friends!

Our family and friends thought we were crazy to believe we could get rich. After all, we could barely pay our bills, we had no special knowledge, skills, or experience. We never went to college, never started our own business, and never made any significant amount of money worth bragging about, so all the odds were definitely stacked against us!

Everything that is, except for one thing...

We had the desire to get rich!

And that was our ace in the hole! We knew that America was the greatest nation on earth and that it was possible for us to get rich! So we started joining all kinds of Network Marketing companies and answering all the get-rich-quick ads we could find!

Now family and friends shook their heads even more in disbelief. "What are you doing?" they'd say. "Why can't you be happy with a regular job?" they asked. "Don't you realize that people like us don't get rich?"

Even though, at first, it looked like our loved ones might be right, we refused to quit, continuing to believe that we could get rich! But, eventually, although we were trying lots (and lots!) of things, we were only getting poorer and started to lose hope, almost giving up many times during the first few years. Nothing was working. We kept digging ourselves deeper into debt, continuing to lose money on almost everything we did. Soon we began to think that our family and friends were right after all – maybe we were losing our minds! Maybe it was crazy to think we could get rich.

But through it all – through all the self-doubts – through all the struggling – one thing saved us: All the great new friends we met at the Network Marketing opportunity meetings! Just like us, these people were dreamers, too! Just like us, they were struggling financially, too. They, too, were ambitious people – people who were hungry for all the great things in life! And because they were determined, nothing was going to stop them!

Well, these people became our new friends! They believed in and supported us, and they assured us that we were not crazy and that everything would turn around for us. if we just "hung in there." This wonderful group of people helped us get out of our depression. Had it not been for them, we would have given up! But because we didn't give up, things turned around for us when we finally discovered the secret that made us over $10 million in our first five years!

So no matter how many problems I have

with Network Marketing, if it were not for the positive, motivated dreamers we met in these Network Marketing companies, we would not be millionaires today.

Because it shows you the possibilities for getting rich, Network Marketing is a great opportunity for people who are just getting started because they have the chance to surround themselves with fellow dreamers who are upbeat, positive, and excited about the endless possibilities – all key ingredients required from people who become a part of, and make up, your support group, people who believe in you and praise you for being so ambitious – because they, too, share the same dreams.

You must surround yourself with people who will lift you up, not tear you down. And if you're lucky, you'll have one or two friends who will stand by you, no matter what. Cling to them! These people are God's gift to you. Thank them for their support and faith in you. Spend more time with them and less time with those who bring you down, those who discourage rather than encourage.

Yes, there are a lot of things wrong with Network Marketing, all of which we'll go over in minute detail in the next chapter. But no matter how much I hate Network Marketing, it doesn't change the fact that...

Some of the Greatest People I've Ever Met Were in These Network Marketing Groups!

While I absolutely abhor most Network Marketing companies, by the same token, I also have a tremendous amount of admiration for most entrepreneurs!

Entrepreneurs are the greatest people on earth! We're the movers and shakers! We want all the best things that life has to offer. We love to build, create, dream, and do big things with our lives! We're optimistic, positive-thinking, upbeat people – all qualities essential for success in business – who are determined to make great things happen!

There are probably millions of entrepreneurs – just like Eileen and me – who got their start in Network Marketing. We all went to similar Network Marketing companies, broke and frustrated, all with a strong desire for (much, much) more, and the ambitious entrepreneurs in these groups took us in, welcoming us with open arms, encouraging us not to give up our dreams, and showing us how to make them happen. Thank God they were there because they truly became our lifesavers! We were drowning in the sea of doubt, but they gave us strength and hope. And when the right opportunity came along, we made millions of dollars in no time flat!

Newer and better Network Marketing companies are coming along everyday that give average people – like you and me – the chance to get rich!

Many of the newer Network Marketing companies are on a mission to combine all of the good things about Network Marketing, at the same time, eliminating the bad. While a number of these companies are better than others, those that are the most sincere should be highly praised.

Yes, Network Marketing is evolving, and in many ways it's getting better because these companies...

   A.   Help the average person make the largest amount of money in the fastest time.

   B.   Are designed to do everything possible

to help the newcomer succeed.

C.   Use Marketing Plans that are easy to understand and simple to use.

D.   Have systems for making money – without bothering your family and friends.

E.   Do not require that you be a salesperson or a public speaker to get rich, you do not have to be a social butterfly – in fact, little or no personal communication is needed to succeed with their Plan. And...

F.   The people behind them truly do care about the average person – not just the heavy-hitters – in their organization.

These are the Network Marketing companies of the future! And thank God for the people behind these true visionaries, a number of whom are ex-distributors for a number of the companies I'll be discussing with you shortly. They know about all the problems of Network Marketing. In fact, most of them are like you and me: They love and hate Network Marketing and are on a mission to build solid companies that take the best of the best of Network Marketing, while eliminating all the bad.

So what separates these companies from all the rest? Well...

A.   Average people make money fast!

With most Network Marketing opportunities, you must build your down-line first (which can take a significant amount of time) before you can make any serious money. Most Network Marketing Plans "pay deep," which means that you must have a lot of people in your group before you can expect to make any money. Meanwhile, you're broke and discouraged and, after a while, you just give up and quit because it takes too long to make any serious money, and you can't afford to wait any longer! And neither can all the people who sign up under you...

The more progressive Network Marketing companies know how difficult it is to get started, so they have special plans to help new distributors make the most money in the least amount of time, which is what builds momentum! New distributors start making money right away – and that gets them even more excited! And making money right away is a very real confidence booster, believe me! It makes you feel great! Now you have something to show for all your faith! It helps people to realize that the Network Marketing opportunity really does have potential. People who are making money don't drop out, and the really smart Network Marketing companies know this, which is why they do everything possible to pay you the largest amount of money in the fastest amount of time!

B.   It's all about the newcomer!

Most Network Marketing opportunities only reward their "heavy-hitters" – the super salespeople who get up and speak before hundreds or thousands of people – the ones who go from city to city and sign up thousands of people within months!

The heavy-hitters can build an Network Marketing company super fast! They are charismatic leaders who know how to motivate large numbers of people, which is why the Network Marketing companies treat them like kings, setting up all kinds of special deals that enable them to make the largest amount of money. Everything is designed to pay big bucks to these super salespeople.

On the other hand, many newer and progressively innovative – AKA smart – Network Marketing companies do everything possible to help the average person make money, too. After all, there are only so many heavy-hitters out there, so these innovative companies understand what I call...

The Weakest Link Theory.

Think of an Network Marketing organization like a chain. Each distributor is a link. If one link is weak, the whole chain is weak. You can have the strongest chain in the world, but if just one link is bad, the whole chain is bad. This is how many of the newer Network Marketing companies think about their organization. Everything is set up to help the average distributor, not the heavy-hitter. The entire company is designed to make it easy for average people to succeed! What a great idea!

C.   Simple and easy compensation plans.

At the very least, because they are so complicated and confusing, you have to be a rocket scientist to understand most Network Marketing compensation plans. Oftentimes, distributors who have been with a company for years still don't understand the plan! As I'll demonstrate in the next chapter, many Network Marketing companies complicate their compensation plans for one reason and one reason only: to help them – not you – make the most money!

New Network Marketing companies are centered around the distributor. Their compensation plans are simple to understand and easy to explain. Most of these plans are focused on helping the average person make the most money – the maximum amount of cash in the minimum amount of time! These new companies do not "pay deep" but, rather, are designed to pay the largest amount of commission to the distributors with the smallest volume of sales – the distributors with the smallest down-lines so that they get the largest amount of money! In other words, they pay the most money to the average distributor, not the super salespeople – those heavy-hitters we just talked about!

These First Three Steps are Changing the Network Marketing Industry Forever!

These new companies know that there are only so many super duper, heavy-hitting salespeople out there, so they do everything possible to build solid companies with people who are not charismatic leaders, public speakers, or super sales types! In other words, these new companies are totally focused on the little guy!

That's right! It's all about helping the

average person make above-average income, which eliminates many of the problems behind most Network Marketing companies. Now average people have the greatest opportunity to succeed! This is our edge, it's our power! Now there is hope for us! We can get started quickly and easily, and have the best chance to make the most money in the shortest amount of time, with the least headaches. At last we're on a solid foundation to build our fortune!

D.   No personal selling!

The majority of Network Marketing companies force you to become a salesperson by either holding home parties or doing face-to-face selling. Well, that's just great if you're a born salesman, but most of us hate selling! In fact, push come to shove, we'd much rather cut off our big toe than make our living trying to sell stuff! Sure, we want to make more money, and we get very excited about the Network Marketing opportunity, but then we find out we have to actually sell the products or services, and that's when we bail out real fast!

So, how can you build a down-line of people who hate to sell? You can't! So the whole idea ends up exploding right in your face!

But, wait. there's more! You see, it's almost impossible to find good salespeople, and most people who are attracted to sales are not stable. I mean, think about it: Sure, they may join your group and make you money for awhile, but then they're gone, moving on to whatever golden opportunity they may consider to be next on their list of things to accomplish. You absolutely cannot build a stable solid down-line with flaky distributors who keep coming and going!

The only way to get steady, dependable

income every month is to have a down-line on which you can depend! And because smart, progressive Network Marketing companies know this, they have developed innovative Marketing Systems that do all the work for you, from recruiting new distributors into your group to selling all the products and services for you and your down-line. Now all your group has to do is work the system, which makes it super easy to attract new distributors who love making money, but hate to sell!

E.   No personal contact!

You have to be a social butterfly to make money with most Network Marketing opportunities. There are all kinds of social functions, award dinners, pep rallies, and motivational seminars. Plus, there are the weekly, and often nightly, opportunity meetings, conference calls you are expected to be a part of, and an endless number of personal phone calls that must be made on a daily basis. Well, if you're a social climber, this is great news indeed! Certainly, we all know people who crave attention. You know the type: They want to be the life of the party and fit in really well in most Network Marketing organizations. In fact, many Network Marketing opportunities are nothing more than social clubs. Although a large percentage of the distributors are not making that much money, they stay in the organization because of the friendships they have formed with other distributors. Undoubtedly, a number of them probably even think that if they hang around long enough, they just might eventually make money!

But there are millions of us who don't crave the spotlight:

✔   We are private people who love to stay home and make money!

✔ We don't want a new group of friends!

✔ We just want to make money!

✔ We don't want to alter our lifestyles!

✔ We don't want to attend pep rallies and motivational seminars!

✔ We hate all the Network Marketing opportunity meetings and training sessions!

✔ We don't even like talking on the phone!

The newer Network Marketing companies know that most individuals would prefer to stay at home and make money, rather than change their lifestyles. And these millions of people don't want to be on the move all the time. Their lives are already much too busy and stressful. They want to sit back, relax, and take it easy.

Because these new companies are in tune with the changing times, they are modernizing the face of Network Marketing by creating opportunities that help millions of us "average" folk – those of us who aren't super salespeople, social butterflies, or public speakers – who simply want a legitimate opportunity to get rich!

F.   Network Marketing companies that really care!

The majority of Network Marketing operators are fueled by greed. The founders of these companies – the ones that are giving Network Marketing a bad rap – don't give a damn about you and me. All they care about is filling up their own bank accounts. They're out to make millions of dollars as fast as possible and really don't care about anything that's long-term. In fact, some of these companies are really criminal organizations that set out to "take the money and run." They sweep the nation (now the world!) like wildfire – some staying only one step ahead of the law at all times – pocket billions, and then go out of business, leaving their distributors high and dry. (Believe me I have a lot more to say about these scumbags in the next chapter!)

However, there's a whole new breed of Network Marketing companies emerging that are totally focused on the long-term and centered around the five elements I discussed in this chapter. It's thanks to them that many of the older companies are forced to either change the way they do business or close their doors for good! I have to say: I love this new trend that's sweeping Network Marketing, and I applaud the new companies – that are the future of Network Marketing – who are doing everything possible to eliminate the worst of Network Marketing while retaining and expanding on the best.

So, as you can see, there are a number of great reasons to "Love Network Marketing!" On the other hand, as you're about to see in the next chapter, there are a lot of reasons to hate Network Marketing, too, but thanks to the progressive, new Network Marketing companies in existence today and on the horizon for tomorrow, there is hope!

CHAPTER TWO

Why Most People Never Make Money in This Business.

And Why You Should Also HATE So Many Things About Network Marketing!

Now it's time to reveal the UGLY TRUTHS about this business. Let's start with the fact that almost nobody ever gets rich in Network Marketing. In fact, they'll be very lucky to bring in even enough cash to pay their bills. Strong words, yes, but if you've been around this industry as long as I have, you know for a fact that it's true!

Taking it one step further, here are two great truths:

1. Because these Network Marketing companies (already) know that most people are not going to make BIG money...

2. They make a nice profit on all the distributors who fail!

Bottom line...

Most folks are just downright doomed!

There's a constant, never-ending parade of Network Marketing distributors who come and go! Frankly, the drop-off rate is huge! Wide-eyed newcomers attend a few meetings or conference calls, get all hyped up, and then fall flat on their faces and quit! They're attracted to Network Marketing like moths to a flame, at first, they get super-excited, but then they burn out just as quickly. and none of us ever see them again!

I don't blame Network Marketing for their never-ending parade of distributors. After all, the cost to join most Network Marketing companies is dirt-cheap, so it truly is "easy-come, easy-go" for many of these newcomers. But I hate the way most Network Marketing companies are not upfront about the fact that very few people make any serious money. It's all just a numbers game with them. The Network Marketing opportunity is like a big meat grinder that puts as many people in as possible and grinds all the money out of them. The big distributors know that the odds are slim that anyone is going to succeed BIG but, of course, they never tell you this.

These companies pretend they care about

you. They try to tell you how special you are to them (but, really, you're not!), and how much you mean to them (but, really, you don't!). It reminds me of the way a politician treats the average citizen. You know who I'm talking about. they move through the crowd, shaking our hands, pretending we're important. But, to them, are we really? No! Absolutely not! The only way we're important to the majority of our political leaders is if we hand them a big fat envelope full of cash every time they shake our hands! You can bet that'll get their attention! Now your vote really counts! And it's the same with Network Marketing. These companies are wolves in sheep's clothing. They pretend to care about the highly-excited newbie who's just getting started. BUT it's all an act! They know that 90% of the new distributors will be gone in less than a year. The people that matter are the movers and shakers who can get up, in front of a crowd, and put a magic spell on everyone else in the room!

So, then, why don't the Network Marketing companies tell you that most people are never going to make any kind of substantial money? Good question, to which the next great truth reveals part or, at least, most of the answer:

Failures = BIG Money!

Network Marketing companies make money... regardless of whether you do or not! These companies are like the giant casinos in Las Vegas that make literally billions of dollars on people (like you and me!) who lose all their money!

Sideline: Here's a Fast Personal Story...

Back in the mid-1980s, I lived in Reno, Nevada, for about a year. I packed all my stuff into a U-Haul trailer and headed west! By the time I pulled into Reno, my car was making some pretty funny noises, so I put it in the nearest repair shop and called a taxi. I told the driver to cruise through some residential areas so I could see the houses. We got a few blocks down the road before he turned to me and said, "Are you new to Reno?" "Yes," said I, somewhat enthusiastically, "I absolutely love this city!" And that's when it happened! This well-meaning taxi driver suddenly had a crazed look in his eyes! He quickly jerked the taxi over to the side of the road and before I could react, was pointing his finger at me, quite angrily, as he shouted: "Stay out of the casinos!" He kept yelling this over and over again for several minutes. I tried to jump out of the car, but the doors were locked. "Let me hear you say it," he shouted. "Say what?" I asked. "Let me hear you say that you will stay out of the casinos." "I will!" I said. "You will what?" he shouted, poking his finger into my chest. "I will stay out of the casinos!" "Say it louder," he insisted. "I will not go into the casinos!" I promised, loudly. All of a sudden he smiled. "Very good," he said, "because those casinos were not built on winners!" Then we pulled back into traffic, almost as though nothing had happened.

This episode only lasted a few minutes, but thanks to him I did very little gambling because his words kept coming back to me...

"Those Casinos Were Not Built on Winners!"

I can't help but think of this crazy cabdriver whenever I meet a wide-eyed newcomer to Network Marketing, which is when I want to shout and scream: "That Network Marketing company wasn't built on the winners!"

And it's true! Most Network Marketing distributors do not succeed, and yet the companies continue to prosper. What's worse is that many of these companies make even more money if you fail! Yes, just like those cushy billion-

AUTOMATIC RECRUITING SYSTEM

dollar casinos, they make more money if you don't succeed, which is one of the main reasons that Network Marketing stinks!

So, here are the top 5 reasons why Network Marketing stinks, big time!

1. With Network Marketing, you are totally dependent on other people.

2. Network Marketing opportunities attract the wrong kinds of people.

3. You must be a charismatic leader or super salesperson to bring in the big bucks.

4. You must be a rocket scientist to understand most Network Marketing marketing and compensation plans.

5. Most Network Marketing companies

make more money if you fail.

Now, let's consider each of these five reasons separately and in combination with each other to prove my point even more about why Network Marketing stinks. big time.

You Cannot Put Your Life in Someone Else's Hands!

The first reason Network Marketing stinks is what I like to call the "dependency factor." Because there are many different angles to this theory, it's a bit complex, but here it is in a nutshell: You cannot – in fact, must not – depend on other people for all your wealth.

On one hand, you do need the help, support, and guidance of other people to make the most money. Yet, on the other hand, your fate is in your hands, and depending on the efforts of others for all your success is a recipe for failure.

People will always let you down. Count on it! A huge part of succeeding big is to take (and accept) the responsibility for your own actions. You cannot depend on other people to make money for you! Otherwise, you're put in a position where you're out of control! To succeed big, you must be in a position of power, and the more control – the better!

If you were to study the lives of the richest people – past and present – you'd find that these individuals have a great degree of control over their fortune. They didn't make it on their own, and while they surround themselves with the best people they can find, they're the ones who are in control. If one of their key people leaves, it's not going to crush them. Network Marketing, on the other hand, can be quite different. Let's say you have a few big distributors in your group who are making you big bucks each month. You're sitting back and making excellent money, while these heavy-hitters do all the work. But then what happens if they leave to join another Network Marketing company?

That's right, they'll take all of their down-line (which is also your down-line) with them. Your income is totally dependent on the big distributors in your group, thus, they become your boss! Your income is totally dependent on them, and if they decide to pull up stakes and move on, your income will dry up really fast! This happens all the time in Network Marketing. Big distributors who have a great deal of influence with their down-line are always being seduced by other Network Marketing companies. These heavy-hitters move around from Network Marketing company to company, taking their loyal flock of distributors with them, which can be a big disaster for you.

So, that's the best case scenario. Usually, however, the real problem is not the big distributors who leave your group but, rather, the fact that you can never find any real movers and shakers to begin with! Yes, it's almost impossible to find dedicated, responsible distributors who will take the business as seriously as you do, so you end up being the only one who's really working hard! All the other people you bring into your down-line are a bunch of deadbeats who don't want to do a damn thing!

Network Marketing attracts wide-eyed dreamers who want to get rich quick – but also want someone else to do everything for them!

Come on, let's face it: There are a lot of lazy people who don't want to put in any effort. If you're like me, you probably know a few of these people, right?

- They lie around a lot and don't want to

do anything!

- They expect someone else to do everything for them!

- They have no motivation!

- They are completely undisciplined!

- They make excuses and whine and cry about how bad they have it!

- They are moochers!

- They look for lazy ways to make a lot of money (that doesn't involve work)!

- They want something for nothing!

Some are big dreamers, and that's great, but they're not doers. Instead, they're always looking for someone else to do everything for them.

**And Many of These Lazy Daydreamers
End Up in Network Marketing!**

Yes, every Network Marketing organization has its share of delusional dreamers who want to get rich quick, without doing a thing. These people are obsessed with the residual income that can be made in Network Marketing. They love the stories of all the big-shot Network Marketing distributors who go to their mailboxes every 30 days and pull out huge checks! They want to be one of these people! But Network Marketing is just a business, and all businesses require a certain amount of time, work, and effort. Network Marketing does give people the opportunity to tap into the power of residual income – but the money doesn't come from doing nothing!

Are the richest people in the world lazy?

Many of the world's richest people hang around at the golf course all day and relax, while other things and people make money for them. But don't let this fool you: Most of these people are reaping the rewards now for something they did in the past...

✔ They built huge companies and sold them for many millions of dollars.

✔ They have a dedicated staff of people who are running their businesses for them.

✔ They are still getting paid for deals they made many years ago.

To reiterate: The money keeps flowing to them because of something they did years ago! Something that now enables them to be able to live out the rest of their days in complete comfort!

What Does This Have to Do with Network Marketing?

AUTOMATIC RECRUITING SYSTEM

Well, that's simple: Network Marketing lets you build a distributor network comprised of other people who can make money for you day and night. Many distributors make the kind of money most doctors and lawyers can only dream of making! This small percentage of Network Marketingers have built a down-line of other distributors who are selling products for them and building their own groups of distributors. They sit back and collect tens of thousands of dollars a month because they built these successful distributor networks.

Some of the richest Network Marketing distributors, who are making millions of dollars a year, live the kind of life that is normally reserved for the very rich and famous. They jet-set around the world, eat in the finest restaurants, stay in the greatest hotels, and shop in the kinds of stores where there are no price tags!

These people have it made in the shade!

They have arrived! Now they are living the lives of celebrities! In fact, many of these individuals are Network Marketing celebrities! They get huge fees for traveling around to all of the Network Marketing conventions around the world, sharing the dream! They get up in front of thousands of success-hungry Network Marketing distributors and share the story of how they became Network Marketing multi-millionaires.

Take a minute to picture yourself at one of those big Network Marketing pep rallies. Thousands of ambitious people are in the crowd as one after another of these Network Marketing millionaires hits the stage, all telling the same stories: How they started out. just like you, how they struggled for years and could barely make it. just like you, but then a miracle occurred, and their lives were changed forever! Suddenly, they discovered the Network Marketing company, and the rest was history! All they did was share the message with a few people who shared it with a few more people who shared it with a few more people who shared it. well, you get the idea. Before they knew it, thousands of dollars were pouring in faster than they could spend it! Now they do nothing, yet the money continues to pour in like crazy!

Can you see yourself listening to these rags-to-riches stories? Good. Now consider this: There is always something missing in all of these stories – all the hard work, sacrifice, dedication, commitment, and persistence these Network Marketing millionaires had to go through to get where they are today!

All of the Effort It Took to Get Rich
Has Been Conveniently Left Out!

The Network Marketing companies mislead people into thinking that getting rich with their opportunity is super easy (it's not!), and they never tell you about the hard work, persistence, sales ability, and other skills their top distributors possess to make the millions they're boasting about. The last thing these companies want you to know is that Network Marketing is a business like any other business. It takes hard work, commitment, and dedication to bring in the big bucks. Sure, some distributors are sitting back and collecting huge sums of money for doing nothing, but these people are simply being rewarded for all the hard work they did to build their down-line. And most Network Marketing millionaires are still working hard! Why? Because building a Network Marketing organization is only part of the work you have to do to get rich in Network Marketing – keeping your down-line producing can take even more work!

And that's another way Network Marketing companies lie to their distributors: They never tell them about all the work they are forced to do to keep their down-line together once it's built.

Because huge numbers of distributors drop out, the people in your down-line must have constant motivation to stay in, and to stay involved. Every 10 distributors who drop out must be replaced with 10 new distributors. It's like a big bucket with holes in the bottom and you're forced to keep filling the bucket!

But wait, that's not your only problem...

There's Still All the Babysitting You're Forced to Do to Get Your Lazy Distributors to Do Anything!

Network Marketing attracts people who haven't given up on their dream for wealth. Unfortunately, many of these folks lack one of the most important qualities of success:

MATURITY!

Being a mature person is one of the major keys to all success. Why? Because mature people take responsibility for their own actions – they are responsible people who know how to take charge of themselves.

- They don't blame other people!

- They don't need someone to tell them what to do!

- They don't whine and cry when things go wrong!

- They don't make a bunch of excuses!

One of the richest people I ever met once told me: "People who are great at making excuses never get rich!"

And boy was he ever right!

People who blame others and make a lot of excuses are weak and immature. They get into the habit of whining and complaining about everything. They find all kinds of things that are wrong – with everything. They focus on all the reasons why they can't do something, instead of looking for the reasons they can and should do it. Come on, this kind of thinking is dangerous to your success! Why? Because whenever you blame other people or focus on all the reasons you supposedly can't do something, what you're really saying is "I'm weak," or "I have no power." After a while, you convince yourself that you are indeed helpless.

The Majority of People Who are New to Network Marketing Have a Lot of Growing Up to Do!

An Network Marketing company is a

business, and many of the people who are new to Network Marketing have never been in business for themselves. They have been employees all their lives. They haven't developed the skills required to think for themselves and take responsibility for their own actions. They don't know how to motivate themselves. Someone else has always done the thinking for them, someone else has always told them what to do. Now they are in your Network Marketing down-line and have the worst person in the world as their boss: Themselves!

Dan Kennedy says: "The best thing about self-employment is that you are your own boss. and the worst thing about self-employment is you are your own boss!" It's true!

Here's another great truth: "The harder you work on yourself – the more money you'll make!"

Remember...

✔ You must grow up to get rich!

✔ You must accept total responsibility for everything!

✔ You must have a solid plan of attack – and then stick to it!

✔ You must get up every morning and do your best!

And, the hardest thing of all:

✔ You must develop persistence to follow through and keep going when the going gets tough! Remember: It's how you handle the adversities that counts.

Anyone can run a business when everything is going smoothly: when the sales and profits are pouring in, or when there are no real problems (except, of course, for: "What do we do with all this money?"), when every day is fun and exciting. These are all great moments, and all a lot of fun. when they actually do happen. In fact, running a successful business is the most incredible feeling on earth! It's exciting to watch your new ideas take off like a rocket! It's thrilling to be around talented people who are just as excited as you, talking about all the ways to make even more money...

But, let's face it. business has its ups and downs, the good versus the bad – a fact that immature people just don't realize because they hate their jobs and are looking for a way out! They naively think that being in business for themselves is the answer to their prayers. Well, these people are delusional. Sure, being self-employed does have its own rewards, but it also has its own penalties, the main one being that you cannot blame anyone else – anymore – ever again – because now that you're self-employed, there's absolutely no one to blame but you! And this can be a real shocker for most people!

So what does all this have to do with why I hate Network Marketing? That's simple: When you're involved with Network Marketing, the people in your down-line are your business partners – and...

Most of Them are Business Partners from Hell!

You end up in business with a whole bunch of people who are as helpless as a newborn baby! They've never been self-employed a day in their lives and, frankly, most of them have no right to even be their own boss! They're unmotivated, immature people who make excuses and will ultimately make your life one living hell guaranteed!

Picture this: You're sick and tired of working for someone else, so you get involved in a red-hot

Network Marketing opportunity. Now you're working your butt off day and night. In fact, you're working harder than ever before – and enjoying every minute of it! This is your destiny! You're on fire with enthusiasm. Then you catch everyone around you on fire, too! Soon you have built a nice down-line of people who want to catch whatever you have! They want to be around you just so some of your warmth and energy will rub off on them! And you're able to fire these people up! You show them the plan, sell them on the vision, and tell them: "Okay, now you go out and do what I'm doing!" What do you think happens next? Yep, you got that right! The whole thing fizzles and falls flat on its face...

"If You Want to Get Rich, You Must Surround Yourself with the Very Best People You Can Find!"

You must have people on your team who are smarter and more talented than you are, strong in all the areas in which you are weak. Unfortunately, finding these people can be very difficult. But find them you must!

People who are new to Network Marketing have the first basic requirement necessary to succeed: The desire to get rich! Well, that's all well and good because without this desire, they'll never make money of any significance. But most of these people lack the other qualities necessary for major success. They demand lots of attention, require constant handholding, and have absolutely no experience in being self-employed!

And what happens the first time something goes wrong? That's right, they quit! They drop out of your group, and you never see or hear from them again!

When these people quit, all the work you put into trying to help them is gone forever. And to make matters even worse, oftentimes, when one person in your group quits, they take two or three other people with them, which can not only be aggravating, but heartbreaking! Now you're back at square one because you have to go out there again to find new distributors for your down-line. Your whole life is spent recruiting new distributors to replace the ones you can't depend on, the ones that drop out. You become burned out and depressed. After all, it's hard enough to motivate yourself, much less all the other people around you, too.

And so it is that after awhile, you can't even stand the people in your down-line! You hate to call them because you know they will only whine and cry or make excuses. Face it. these people are not self-starters like you, and they will never work as hard as you do because they are not driven to succeed. Oh, sure, they may be dreamers, but they are not doers, which is why they drop out of your group the very first time they realize that they must actually do something to make money!

The Network Marketing Vortex!

There is nothing worse than being surrounded by people you can't rely on, which is why many successful Network Marketing distributors finally say, "That's it! Enough is enough!" So they finally quit, get out of what my friend Ken Pedersen calls "The Network Marketing Vortex," and start another business where the amount of money they make is not dependent on other people.

But, in some cases, the nightmare they went through in Network Marketing ends up becoming a very positive thing for these distributors because they end up achieving major success in other businesses where they have complete control over the money they make. Network Marketing taught them many things such as the value of other people who help them get rich. But now these other people who are helping them are their employees! And when one of them is not carrying their weight, they can be fired on the spot only to have 10 more people standing in line begging for the job! Now they are in control of their own destiny!

I have tried to depict an accurate picture of the nightmare that many Network Marketing distributors are faced with on a daily basis. It can be a living hell! Your whole business becomes dependent on unreliable people. Oh, sure, while a number of them are well-meaning, they cannot (better put, definitely should not!) be self-employed because they lack the skills necessary for success.

Network Marketing is a people business, and even the best will let you down. You must have strong people you can count on, those who don't need constant care and supervision, because they're the ones who become the strong links in your chain. Unfortunately, these people are few and far between. Unfortunately, the very best are usually impossible to get because they're already living their dream, and they would never consider joining your down-line anyhow because they're too absorbed in their own highly successful careers.

I hate Network Marketing because your entire business is dependent on weak people – the ones who constantly let you down – who will never come as close to working as hard as you do.

Bottom line...

One Thousand Weak People, Together,
Will Never Equal One Strong Person!

But wait! All is not lost because there are a

number of people – perhaps one in a million – who always make money in Network Marketing! So much so, in fact, they're jet-setting multi-millionaires! They go from one Network Marketing company to another, making huge sums of money with little to no effort! But, remember...

To Get Rich in Network Marketing, You Must Be a World-Class, Superstar Salesman!

But, realistically speaking, most people would rather eat a can of live worms than try to sell something! That's right, they hate to sell and would do whatever it takes to avoid trying to persuade someone into buying anything, which is bad news for those who want to get rich in Network Marketing. Why? Because Network Marketing is a sales and distribution game – oh, yeah, sure, the Network Marketing companies try to skate over this issue by telling you that you don't have to be a super salesman to get rich with their opportunity. Just not true, and all you have to do is spend a little time with their most successful distributors to know that.

Go to any Network Marketing pep rally and rub shoulders with these millionaire bigwigs, and I guarantee that you'll see what truly super salespeople they are. They're charismatic leaders who crave the spotlight, skilled motivators who know how to get hundreds of people so excited they almost pee in their pants, and dynamic speakers who can hypnotize an audience of millionaire wannabees out of all their money! These people are not like you and me. they're magical, full of charisma! There's a certain, powerful energy about them that you can almost feel when they enter a room. All heads turn to look at them, they light things up wherever they go, they're magnetic! People just want to get around them. and stay there!

So, you might ask yourself: Were these

Network Marketing millionaires born with their special abilities? Can you develop these qualities in yourself? And even if you could, do you really want to? Are you the kind of person who can get up and dazzle large groups of people – or – do you hate public speaking? Do you want to be a skilled salesperson who can sell refrigerators to Eskimos – or – do you hate the idea of trying to get people to hand over their money? Do you crave the spotlight, attention and power, want to be famous? Or do you just want to sit back quietly, getting rich from the comfort of your home? Well, depending on how you answered these questions, perhaps you'll be one of these famous Network Marketing celebrities or even the next Network Marketing dynamo multimillionaire!

But Most People Don't Want to Be a Sales Superstar!

The majority of Network Marketing companies

hide the truth about all the qualities it takes to make millions of dollars. They know full well that only one-tenth of their distributors will make any substantial money. But do they care? Since they're making money whether you make money or not, what do you think? They put the carrot out there for all of us to chase! The lure of making millions is always there, ever-looming! They keep the dream of "millionaireship" alive inside us, even though they know full well that we'll fall flat on our faces.

Come on, let's be realistic here. you absolutely cannot – no, will not. become an Network Marketing millionaire without being a world-class leader, salesperson, and public performer. And for you to think otherwise is ludicrous! Frankly, it makes me mad as hell when I think of all the people out there who believe they actually have a chance to stay home, lead a semi-normal, quiet life, and get rich in Network Marketing. Forget about it! It just "ain't gonna" happen! You're better off with a thick stack of lottery tickets you can scratch while sitting in front of the TV. In fact, if you want a quiet, hassle-free life, that's probably what you should do...

Because If You Want to Get Rich in Network Marketing, Your Entire Life is Going to Turn Upside Down!

To get rich in Network Marketing requires a blur of never-ending activities: the won't-they-ever-stop phone calls, opportunity meetings, pep rallies, and all kinds of social functions – all great stuff if you're an extrovert who loves to be surrounded by lots of people wherever you go. But what if you're not? What if your idea of having a great time doesn't even remotely include being the life of the party? What if you love to spend quiet time with your family and friends? What if you dread social functions? Or what if you're a quiet person who believes in the old adage that "Less is more."? (And, remember, you've got to ask yourself these questions before you decide if Network Marketing is right for you.)

You see, with Network Marketing, you never really know what you're getting yourself into – until it's too late. Once you're in, of course, you eventually discover the truth but by then, there's nothing you can do about it! Now you have spent a few years working your butt off and you're making just enough to quit your job and pay the bills, so you should be feeling great, correct? After all, you're living the American dream, right? But are you feeling great? No! Why? Because your Network Marketing business is a living nightmare and you find that you're even more trapped than ever before! Why? Because you don't have a business, in fact, all you have is...

The Job from Hell!

Because you hate what you have to do to

make your money, and yet you're making just enough money where you can't quit! Now you're really trapped! You started your Network Marketing business because you wanted to be free, but know that's far from the truth. Now you're an Network Marketing prisoner! Each and every day you are forced to get out of bed and do all the things you hate to do, including (albeit only briefly) the following:

- You've got to make 100 phone calls a day to motivate your troops.

- You must worry about such things as...

- Your key distributors, who are constantly being seduced by other Network Marketing companies.

- The lack of sales from your down-line.

- People in your group who aren't

133

willing to do a damn thing!

It's the job from hell because you have the constant, never-ending pressure of keeping all the distributors in your group motivated and happy! You must always worry about your key distributors, the people who are making you all the money. Will they stay in your group, or be seduced by another Network Marketing company? Are they happy, or secretly plotting against you? Will they leave your group and take the key people in their down-lines with them to join some hot, new "ground floor" opportunity? They might! In fact, this happens all the time.

Okay, picture this: You have 5 main distributors who are real movers and shakers. These people are winners, not whiners! All 5 of them are working their butts off! They're recruiting machines, and you're as happy as a puppy with a box of squeeze toys! After all, this is the dream of Network Marketing, right? You bet!

Now you have a handful of super-talented distributors who are making you a ton of money! These 5 winners are like money in the bank for you! They're making a ton of money for themselves, and you're getting a piece of every dollar they make! And they just keep right on making more and more money! Their down-lines are exploding with growth, and you keep getting richer! Soon these 5 dynamic leaders have attracted their own Network Marketing superstars! So, what does this mean? Simply put, now you're in the solid position to become a millionaire! In fact, you're so close to being rich you swear to yourself that you can almost taste it!

Each month your checks get bigger and bigger as your 5 key superstars weave their magic! Now you're living the Network Marketing dream: Your checks are growing bigger by the month, and you're not doing anything extra! Now you can afford to do all the things you have always wanted to do because all the money you have ever wanted is pouring in and you have lots of time to spend it. Now you can sit back and relax, right? Beep! Wrong!

Because Your Million-Dollar Network Marketing Empire Can Come Crashing Down in Only a Matter of Days!

It's true that the top Network Marketing distributors are few and far between, therefore, if you're a super – successful, Network Marketing distributor, the word will quickly spread, and people will know about you. Your name will be well-known by all of the Network Marketing insiders, and everyone will want you! You'll start getting calls from other Network Marketing millionaires who will invite you to all kinds of closed-door meetings and gatherings in some of the most exotic places!

They'll offer to "stop by" in their private jet and whisk you away for an all-expense paid, mini-vacation to their secret hideaway.

This small group of Network Marketing millionaires will try to seduce you away from the company you're with because that's how they get rich! In fact, the true secret of the richest people in Network Marketing is that...

They Spend All of Their Time Making All Kinds of Special Deals to Lure Heavy-Hitters Away!

Oh, but wait. there's more...

If you were the owner of a Network Marketing company and all you had to do was cut a special deal to one big Network Marketing superstar to quickly get 1,000 or 5,000 or even 25,000 of his top distributors, wouldn't you? You bet you would! And that's the kind of thing that happens in Network Marketing – the richest and most successful distributors are being courted and seduced by all the greedy Network Marketing companies who will do almost anything to get them! And that's great if you are one of these Network Marketing superstars because, after all, being on the receiving end of one of these deals – to get everything from all kinds of special cash advances, stock options, and signing bonuses – could be worth literally millions to you! And the more of your key distributors who make the move with you, the more money goes into your bank account! Why, this can be your ticket to the millions you seek!

Again, all of this is absolutely fantastic if you're the Network Marketing superstar who's being chased by all the other top Network Marketing companies and distributors. But what if the person being courted is one of a handful of your key distributors? What then? Well, I'm sure you probably guessed already, and you're right. Within a few short weeks, everything you spent years to build can come crashing down. All of your top distributors can leave you – very, very quickly – and take each and every one of their best people with them, leaving you right back where you started, with all of your income quickly drying up in no time at all.

You Must Be a Brilliant Rocket Scientist or Brain Surgeon to Understand Most Network Marketing Compensation Plans!

Network Marketing compensation plans are complicated primarily because they help the company make more money! Think about it: These companies do not want their distributors to understand exactly how you're getting paid. For example, if your check is $1,297 less than it was last month, they can confuse you with all the complexities of their plan and convince you there's a good reason. They are in complete control, not you, and since your distributor agreement says the company can terminate your membership at any time, you'd better not challenge them too hard.

If Network Marketing companies really want to help you make the most money, why are their compensation plans (i.e., the way they pay their distributors) so complicated? The answer is simple: They do it because it's in their best interests. Simple compensation plans are easily challenged. You can instantly spot where the company made a mistake. But the complicated plans are basically designed to intimidate you. After all, how can you question the amount of money they're paying you if you don't even understand the way you're being paid? And how can you possibly know if you're being treated fairly or even if you're getting all the money that should be coming to you?

You can't. They have all the control and power, and you have none. After all, if your check seems smaller than it should be, that's your problem, not theirs.

These Network Marketing compensation plans are similar to the income tax we pay on the money the government lets us keep. In fact, the rules and regulations of how much money we owe the government is so complicated, accountants and CPAs must go to special schools each year just to keep up with all the new laws. There has been a lot of talk about a simpler tax code, such as a flat tax where, if you make $50,000 a year, you pay $10,000, and, if you make $250,000 a year, you pay $50,000, which sounds great! Now all of us can quickly know how much money we owe the government by simply multiplying the amount of money we make by the percentage of our tax and then cutting Uncle Sam a check! What a novel idea!

AUTOMATIC RECRUITING SYSTEM

But the flat tax will never happen! No way, Jose! Forget about it! You see, there's no way we'll ever have a simple income tax policy because there are too many people who profit from the complicated version. And all of these people must keep things complicated so they can keep their cushy jobs. And just think about all the people who would lose their high-paying jobs if we had a simple flat tax...

- Accountants/CPAs

- Lawyers

- Financial Consultants and Advisors

- And most of the IRS Agents!

These people make big bucks by keeping the amount of money you owe the U.S. Government as complicated as possible! There's no way they'll ever stand by and let something like a flat tax happen because it's in their best interests – not ours – to keep the tax code as complicated as possible. In fact, the more complex it is the better. Now they can make more money by "helping you and me pay the lowest taxes." Well, I don't think so!

Come on, think about it: The people they're helping is them, not us! And what really makes me mad are all of the lawyers and accountants and financial advisors who talk out of both sides of their mouths. When you're in their office, they'll agree with you that the current income tax policies are too damn complicated. They nod their heads that there should be a simple and easy way to pay your taxes. But they're lying because when they get together with their buddies, all they do is sit around and schmooze about all the newest laws that will make them more money. Come on, they don't care about you! The last thing they want is for things to be simple and easy. After all, if that were the case, who would need their services?

Most Network Marketing compensation plans are like the I.R.S. Tax Code – absolutely impossible to understand! Do you really want to stake your financial future on a compensation plan that is so complicated you need a team of accountants to understand it? I don't think so!

The majority of Network Marketing compensation plans are designed to reward the company and its biggest distributors first, and that would be okay if they were upfront about this, but they're not. They lie to you, just like the greedy politician lies to try to get your vote. There's a lot of talk about helping the "average" distributor make the most money, but talk is cheap. And when you see a compensation plan that's loaded with all kinds of complicated crap, you can be sure that it's not designed to help the average individual.

But, hey, don't get me wrong! I certainly can't blame the Network Marketing companies for looking out for their own interests. After all, if it were your company you, too, would be trying to do everything possible to reward your most productive distributors in the greatest way possible. So all this makes a lot of sense. In fact, it's even necessary. But what bothers me (and should upset you a lot, too) is the way these companies try to camouflage their true intentions, much like the politician who knows it's impossible to cut the taxes of the country's middle-class citizenry and yet gets in front of all the TV cameras and lies about his intentions nonetheless, just to get our votes.

But the lies many Network Marketing companies cover up go even deeper than the way they pay their distributors because...

Network Marketing Companies
Make More Money If You Fail!

And that's probably one of the biggest reasons why I hate Network Marketing!

Actually, the real goal of most Network Marketing companies is not to help their distributors get rich. Most Network Marketing companies are forced to create all kinds of special opportunities for their heavy-hitters. The more they pay to this small group of guys and gals, the less money they get. So the only way they can make their money is on the large group of semi-successful distributors who never get rich – the ones who make just enough money to not drop out!

Bottom line...

The Little Guy Always Gets Screwed!

Even in Network Marketing, by:

1.   Compensation plans that pay too deep.

2.   Compensation Plans with breakaways.

3.   Companies that make more money if you fail!

And the more you know about all three of these pitfalls, the more you'll hate Network Marketing, too! So, let's cover them one at a time...

The "Pay Deep" Rip-Off Plan...

Most Network Marketing plans pay you on 7 to 15 levels of distributors beneath you. They try to tell you that if you get a handful of good distributors and they do the same, eventually you'll have tens of thousands of people below you, and a small percentage of every sale will trickle back up to you. Sounds great, doesn't it? All you have to do is get 5 people who get more, and on and on, so that you'll soon have thousands of people below you, which means that your working days are over! Now you're on Easy Street! Just go to your mailbox every month and pull out your big, fat check because...

Now You're Making Tens of Thousands of Dollars a Month While Others Do All the Work!

I got so excited the first time a friend showed me how Network Marketing was supposed to work that I can still vividly remember leaving his house at in the early morning hours, so excited I could hardly keep my van on the road! I just knew I was going to be a millionaire in no time flat! Oh, yeah, the good life was out there, and all I had to do was go out and find 5 people to find 5 people to find 5 more, and so on and so forth. Soon, I'd be the king of my own Network Marketing Empire and thousands of people would be making money for me! I'd spend my life jet-setting around the world, living the kind of life we see in the movies!

The possibilities were endless! I had finally discovered the true secret to wealth! Now all I had to do was sell the dream to 5 more people just like me and let them do the same! Soon I'd have my own private island somewhere in the South Pacific! Yeah, right!

Well, if you've ever heard a great Network Marketing presentation, you know just what I'm talking about – it's pretty heady stuff, I can tell you! The skilled presentations are spellbinding! And much of what they say is even true, for instance, the talk about the excessive markups from the manufacturers to the end consumer, and how the Network Marketing company takes that money and spreads it around to all of its distributors. It sounds almost like Robin Hood, doesn't it? The "take from the rich and give to the poor" idea is very appealing.

And Network Marketing also does a great job of educating people on the true secret of getting rich: leverage! For the first time in your life, you realize that getting paid by the hour is the worst possible way to make money. You come face to face with certain truths about getting rich. One that stays with me to this day is J. P. Getty's famous quote:

> "I'd Rather Make 1% from the Efforts of 100 Men, Than 100% from My Own Effort."

I first learned that secret at an Amway meeting and, boy, did it ever change my life!

Network Marketing teaches you how to

build a distribution business where you get paid on many things, other than your time. This is the secret to getting rich! But the Pay Deep Plan is a scam! It's a total rip-off because the whole idea that you are going to bring in 5 people who each bring in 5 who bring in 5 more is total, absolute nonsense! It's mathematically impossible! Want proof! Okay, consider this...

Let's pretend you're part of one of these Pay Deep scams, and you're getting paid on 13 levels. And let's also say that your plan is to get 6 distributors who go out and get 6 more... Sounds easy, doesn't it? After all, everyone knows 6 people, right? And all you're doing is giving these 6 people the opportunity of a lifetime, correct? Now who in their right mind could resist that? So you go out and show 6 of your friends how they can get rich. You show them how stupid they are to get paid by the hour at some dead-end job and get them to sign-up with you. Now you have your 6, and you're on your way to Easy Street!

AUTOMATIC RECRUITING SYSTEM

So you help your 6 friends get their 6, and then you teach your 6 friends how to help their 6 find 6, and then you teach them how to teach their people, and sure enough, their 6 distributors also go out and get their own small group! Whew! Soon you have hundreds of people in your group, and you never signed up more than your first 6! After that, all you had to do was show them to duplicate your efforts, etc. and so forth.

Now you have hundreds of people making money for you! The dream is real! Here's what your group looks like:

Levels / Number of Distributors in Your Group

LEVELS	NUMBER OF DISTRIBUTORS IN YOUR GROUP
1st	6
2nd	36
3rd	216
4th	1,296

Yes, in just a short time, you have over 1,000 people who are making you money! And what did you have to do to get this money? Well, that's the greatest part! You simply got 6 of your friends to sign up 6 of their friends! Each person in the group then sells just a tiny amount of the product to at least 10 other people a month. That's it! It's so simple! And yet the numbers are there to prove it's real! By the sixth month, your group is four levels deep, and the total number of distributors is 1,554! And if each of them sells $100 worth of product a month to 10 of their neighbors or relatives, how much money would that be? Well, here, let's do the math:

1,554 total distributors (4 levels deep)

x 10 customers

= 15,540 total customers

x $100 per month in sales

= $1,554,000.00

Your little Network Marketing distribution

center is doing $1,554,000.00 in monthly volume! Many of the local stores in your city that have been in business for years aren't even making that kind of money! And it seems so simple! After all, the numbers are there in black and white. You don't have to be a math whiz to see that 6 distributors who get 6, who get 6, who get 6 = 1,554 total distributors. And if each one sells $100 worth of product a month to only 10 others, your total distributor volume is $1,554,000.00 a month. Even if you're only getting 7% of that money, it still comes out to...

$108,780.00 a Month!

You're making $108,780.00 a month and just getting started! In fact, you're only 4 levels deep, and your Network Marketing company pays on 13 levels. And the thing that's most compelling is that you actually see the numbers! They draw the plan out for you and the message is so amazing!

Here's how it's supposed to work...

- Each distributor only does a very small amount of work (very small)...

- You simply sign up no more than 6 people...

- And teach them how to duplicate the process...

- Then you and each distributor only sells a small amount of the product to no more than 10 retail customers...

Oh, my God, it's so simple! And the numbers prove that this can be an amazing form of distribution! It seems so "American," doesn't it?! Why pay all those layers of middlemen? Why not just get it straight from the manufacturer and let the people split the profits? It almost makes you want to jump up and chant "Power to the People!" over and over again! The fact that you can actually see the numbers makes it believable and, oh, so compelling – after all, numbers don't lie, right?

Well, here are some numbers the Pay Deep Network Marketing companies won't show you – numbers that prove that the whole thing is a scam!

Let's go back to the "Get 6 who get 6 more" diagram to see just how many people you're going to make money on (but, get prepared because the answer is shocking)!

NUMBER OF LEVELS	NUMBER OF DISTRIBUTORS IN YOUR GROUP (If all 6 get 6 more.)
1	6
2	36
3	216
4	1,296
5	7,776
6	46,656
7	279,936

8	1,679,616
9	10,077,696
10	60,466,176
11	362,797,056
12	2,176,782,336
13	13,060,694,016

As you can see, if you were paid on 13 levels of only 6 distributors who get 6 more, you'd have over 15 billion people in your group! But that's impossible! After all, that would include every man, woman, and child in the entire world. and then some! After all, there are less than 6 billion people on the planet!

The example I've just given you is fictional. These days, only the most illegal pyramid schemes that try to pass themselves off as legitimate Network Marketing opportunities tell you they pay on unlimited numbers of distributors. But there are still plenty of "Matrix Style" Network Marketing opportunities that promise to pay you for 2 distributors who get 2 more, and many of these companies claim they'll pay you all the way to 15 levels! Do the math, and you'll see what a scam that is!

The whole idea behind "pay deep" is a rip-off, and yet the world is full of die-hard Network Marketingers who refuse to see the truth. These people are not ignorant. They can clearly see that 13 levels of 6 distributors each comes out to over twice the population of the entire globe. But their brains are full of greed. Even though they know it can never happen, they still think it's possible to get rich if only a few distributors on each level do something!

The Network Marketing companies keep pushing their "we're going to pay you a little percentage of the money on a lot of levels" approach because they know it doesn't work!

Nobody ever builds their down-line to the deeper levels, so the company never has to pay 99% of its distributors this money. In fact, the only people who get paid on these deeper levels is the company! But a lot of companies have created a more "businesslike" model – called the "Breakaway Plan" – that certainly doesn't look like an illegal chain letter at all but is loaded with myriad problems nonetheless.

And what's the main problem with most Breakaways? It's simple: If the distributors you bring into your group do better than you, they will breakaway from your group, in which case you won't make a dime on them anymore! Picture this: You bring in a few, really great distributors. You bust your butt to help them build their down-lines. And your help pays off! Now all three of these distributors are on fire! They're building their down-lines as fast as a new casino gets built in Vegas!

Okay! So now you can sit back and get

rewarded for all your hard work, right? Beep! Wrong! Because now if these three winners begin outperforming you, they'll breakaway from your group, and when this happens, you'll stop making a penny on all the business they generate!

Now, what kind of crap is that!?

The Network Marketing companies give you all kinds of reasons why they must have these breakaways, but it's all a pack of lies. The real reason they have these plans is to make sure you never stop working your butt off! The dream of sitting back and letting other people make money for you is nothing but a fantasy. fiction. a sham. zilch. nada. it's all smoke and mirrors! Come on, the last thing these companies want to do is pay people for doing nothing!

So add up all these facts and figures, and you'll hate Network Marketing as much as I do!

And remember: 1. Not every Network Marketing company is a scam, and 2. each company has its own type of compensation plan, some of which are really quite unique. But you have to be a full-time student of Network Marketing to understand all the variations of the way these outfits promise to pay their distributors. And here's a tip: Ignore all compensation plans that pay you a little money on a lot of levels. Your chances of getting hit by lightning are far greater than building a huge down-line with 12 to 15 levels of distributors.

So now you've seen some of the "ugly" side of the Network Marketing business. I hope this has been an eye-opening experience. But wait. There's one last Chapter in this Section. Read it and I'll reveal the #1 reason why most people never make a lot of money in this business. Then, in the last 2 Sections, I'll make sure that YOU will NEVER be one of these people!

CHAPTER THREE

The #1 Reason Why Network Marketing Does Not Work for the Average Man or Woman.

The recruiting methods most Network Marketing companies and trainers teach are completely un-duplicatable. This Chapter tells you why. As you'll see, this is the main reason that most people do NOT make any significant amounts of money.

So let's begin...

For starters, duplication is your key to getting rich. There are almost 10,000,000 millionaires in this country right now – and all of them have used some form of duplication to make their fortunes.

This includes the tens of thousands of people who have become rich in Network Marketing.

Yes, in spite of all the problems I've told you about in this book, there are still thousands of people who have managed to get rich in Network Marketing. The #1 reason they have achieved this wealth is due to the power of duplication.

Here's how I define this principle:

"The power of duplication is any system
of making money that does not
require your direct continual efforts."

There are many different ways people are using the power of duplication to get rich. Here's a simple example to show you one way you could do it:

Let's say you want to use the power of duplication to get rich in the retail business. This is an area that has made many people millions of dollars: 1. You would open up your first store, learn all you could, and get it profitable. 2. You would teach someone else how to run the store for you. 3. You would take the profits from the first store and start a second one in another location. 4. You would get it profitable and train someone else to run it. 5. Then you would simply duplicate your efforts and start a 3rd, 4th and 5th store.

It's such a simple money-making formula.

Assuming all your stores were profitable – you could be making money on 7, 10, or even 20 stores at once – with very little extra effort on your part.

You Could Actually Sit Back –
Let Someone Else Supervise Everything –
and Make Millions of Dollars a Year!

AND THIS IS EXACTLY HOW Network Marketing IS SUPPOSED TO WORK! The people who have become rich in the business have utilized this powerful get-rich principle.

Here is how you are told you can get rich:

1.   You buy the company's products at wholesale and sell them at retail (just like a store operates). The retail profit is yours to keep.

2.   Your "up-line" (the various layers of distributors in your sales organization) are paid a percentage of your

"wholesale volume." This is how they make their money from your efforts.

3. Then, you train another person to do what you do. They buy the product at wholesale and sell it at retail. You get a percentage of their business.

4. Then, they duplicate your efforts. – They train others to do the exact same thing you taught them how to do.

5. Those people duplicate the process too and before long...

You Can Have Hundreds of
Distributors in Your Group
Who are Making You Money!

The top Network Marketing distributors who are making $30,000, $50,000 and even $100,000 a month or more are able to earn these incredible sums because they are getting paid a percentage of the business that is generated by hundreds of people.

The Network Marketing companies tell you that anyone can get rich following this exact formula. That's a lie. You see, after studying hundreds of compensation plans and interviewing hundreds of unsuccessful distributors, I am absolutely convinced that:

Your Chances of Getting Rich
with Traditional Recruiting
Methods are Slim to None.

In fact, you have a greater chance of walking outside of your home in a thunderstorm and getting struck by lightning than you do of ever getting rich in most Network Marketing opportunities.

The reason is simple: The traditional

recruiting methods most companies and their trainers teach are completely and totally unduplicatable for the average person.

If these methods are completely unduplicatable for the average person – then guess who makes all the money? That's right, it's the super sales people, the public speakers, the motivators, hustlers and – of course – the companies themselves. Think about this.

All of the successful distributors we've ever met and studied fit a certain profile. They are full of enthusiasm. They can get up in front of a crowd of people and get everyone excited. They aren't afraid to sell. Most even enjoy it.

These top distributors have a lot in common with politicians. They are very skilled at "working a group." They enjoy meeting people. They love the spotlight. They love being leaders and getting lots of attention. They are comfortable in front of big crowds. They are entertainers. They can get in front of a group of people and tell them what they want to hear. They have the gift of gab!

The best politicians in the world are hustlers. They are salespeople. They love shaking lots of hands and "selling" their ideas to others. They are good at telling different groups of people what they want to hear. Some are even great liars and cheaters. All of them enjoy the POWER of their positions and they love the game of climbing to the top!

Here's what I want you to do: Think of the most street-smart/hustler you know of. Someone really ruthless. Can you do this? (Of course, you can!) Now, take the image of that person and realize that this is the type of person you must become to be a top distributor and earn tens of thousands of dollars a month! This is...

The #1 Reason Network Marketing
Does Not Work for the
Average Man or Woman.

The average man or woman has nothing in common with a politician who craves power and attention. – He or she is not a super salesperson or public speaker.

The average man or woman does not enjoy doing the kinds of things it takes to get rich in this business:

- They hate having to sell things to other people.

- They hate having to go to "opportunity meetings."

- They hate having to try to constantly recruit their friends and family members.

- They hate having to try to recruit all of their past acquaintances.

- They hate having to drag unwilling people to opportunity recruiting meetings or trying to sell them products or services these people don't want.

- They hate trying to convince people of anything.

- They hate having to take advantage of the people they know.

- They hate having to give up their quiet time at home with their families or friends to go out and try to sell things to people.

- They hate having to change their entire lives in order to try to recruit distributors or sell products.

- And they are absolutely terrified to get up in front of a group of strangers at an opportunity meeting and attempt to sell to them or motivate them.

AND THESE ARE THE THINGS YOU HAVE TO DO TO GET RICH IN Network Marketing!

Can you see why it is totally unduplicatable?

HERE IS THE NO-WIN FORMULA	
You must do everything I've just mentioned.	But 97% of the people you try to recruit absolutely <u>hate</u>.
They may try it for a while, but they don't make enough money – and after a while they quit and give up.	And the only people who end up making it are the super salespeople who filter up to the top.

97% of the people who become involved in Network Marketing can't stand the pain of doing

AUTOMATIC RECRUITING SYSTEM

the things they have to do to make money with this form of marketing. They become discouraged and quit. This makes me angry because:

1. The companies are dishonest with these people. They lure them into their organizations without telling them all that they will have to do or become or give up in order to make the type of income they promise.

2. These people are being cheated. They are being taken advantage of by these companies who make money from their efforts knowing that there's a 97% (or better) chance that they will fail.

The Network Marketing companies have set everything up in their favor – so they can make their money – even though 97% don't succeed.

Have you been one of these 97% who have

failed? If so, did you ever stop to realize that your failure was not your fault?

As for me, I felt like a loser. I thought the reason I couldn't make it in this industry was my fault. I blamed myself totally for not having what it took to build a downline. I was angry at myself for the way I was living my life: Getting involved in an Network Marketing company – throwing myself into it – working hard for a few weeks or months – and then becoming frustrated and quitting.

What I never realized was that there were millions of people just like me who couldn't make it in Network Marketing and that the companies knew our success was almost impossible.

These Companies Have
Lied to You and Me.

They taught us about the principles of

duplication. They showed us how much money we could possibly make if we just had enough people in our downlines. They got us excited about building a group of distributors and making money from the efforts of many different people. And they got us thinking about all of the many thousands of dollars we could make. They got us to dream of having all kinds of nice things that money and freedom can buy.

BUT THEY DIDN'T TELL US WE HAD TO BECOME SUPER-SALESPEOPLE TO GET RICH!

- They didn't tell us that we were going to have to go out every single day and face the major rejection of people telling us they didn't want what we were selling.

- Or that we were going to have to get up in front of groups of people and try to persuade them to join the company.

- Or that we were going to have to learn how to do sales "presentations."

- Or to learn how to be sales trainers and teach the people we sponsored how to sell the products and the program.

- Or that we were going to have to take advantage of all of our friendships and acquaintances by trying to convince them to join.

- Or that we were going to have to give up a big part of our lives and dedicate it to the Network Marketing company – while we were still holding on to our regular employment.

- Or that our chances of failing were so

great that it would have been a sure bet for anyone gambling on us.

- And the worst part of all: They didn't tell us that – because of all these things – the odds were totally against us of ever making any serious money with their plan. And that they were going to make big profits on us. Even though we failed.

THE BOTTOM LINE: Millions of people's lives like yours and mine are ruined because of all of this deceitfulness and dishonesty. We get involved in these Network Marketing plans without knowing what we are getting involved in, or all the things it really takes to be successful.

You and I have been lied to by these companies. They lure us into their opportunities with the hope of making thousands of dollars a month – without telling us all we will have to do to get it. If you've ever experienced this for yourself, then you know exactly what I'm talking about. If not, then consider yourself lucky because the pain of getting your hopes up, thinking your whole life is going to change and then failing miserably is the most terrible pain you can ever experience.

I've told you a little about our own struggle and painful experiences with many different Network Marketing companies. I am very upset that we were lied to by these companies, but as I have told you in other parts of this book: there is one thing I'm very happy about.

These Companies Helped Us Realize
That It Was Possible For Average People
Like Us To Get Super Rich!

Because of this, we continued to search for the ultimate way to get rich. This lead to the powerful wealth-making secret you'll read about in the next Section of this book. It's called: 'Direct Response Marketing' and, as you'll see, this was the golden key I used to make as much as $100,000 a month without any personal selling. It can be your secret to getting rich in Network Marketing, too! To find out how, please go to the next Section now!

SECTION TWO

How Our Methods are Designed to Make You HUGE SUMS of Money Without Talking to a Single Person!

In this Section I will reveal the secret that has let me and a small group of other lucky people make a fortune in Network Marketing with zero personal selling and without any of the headaches and hassles most distributors are going through.

CHAPTER FOUR

How to Make Thousands of Dollars a Month in Network Marketing with Zero Rejection!

As you (hopefully) know by now, a good Marketing System gives you the power to:

1.   Reach many thousands of prospects who are perfect for your Network Marketing opportunity and repel all of

the people who will only end up wasting your time and cause you heartaches and pain.

2.   Attract people who are ready to get started now.

3.   Avoid talking to anyone. If you do personally talk to anyone (your choice!) it will only be to those people who are most serious, already 100% sold and ready to start making you big money!

With this proven System, you can make huge sums of money in Network Marketing without any of the headaches and hassles most people suffer through!

Does all of this sound too good to be true? It's not! And if you'll keep an open mind and study what I have to teach you – you'll be in for quite a surprise! How big of a surprise? Well, the first time I used these methods in a Network Marketing program, I made...

$234,795.00 in Less Than 9 weeks!

That's right – I used the same no-rejection methods I am freely sharing with you how to bring in almost a quarter of a million dollars in less than 9 weeks from the day I started!

How's that for proof?

How would you like to do this?

Can you see it?

I hope so! Because, with the secrets in this book, you can.

I don't tell you my story to brag. It's not

AUTOMATIC RECRUITING SYSTEM

about me. It's about the success I've achieved with these methods. The best part is the fact that...

All of this money was made in 9 weeks without me personally having to talk with a single person or personally having to "sell" anything to anyone!

So what are the marketing methods that made me all this money? Well, what I have been mastering since 1988 is an often misunderstood form of marketing known as 'Direct Response.'

Direct Response Marketing is responsible for billions of dollars in sales each year! However, it is also a highly misunderstood form of marketing because it has many variables that are hidden from the novice. In other words...

There are thousands of little-known tips, tricks, and strategies (that are used by the masters of Direct Response Marketing) that only a small group of people truly understand. Those who do can achieve huge results like I did when I applied these methods to a Network Marketing opportunity.

I simply took the knowledge and skills in Direct Response that I had spent many years developing – put it into a Network Marketing opportunity – and presto! Many thousands of dollars started pouring in like a raging river of cash! That's the awesome power behind this form of marketing...

This Often Misunderstood Form of Marketing Can Bring in Large Sums of Money So Fast You Won't Believe It!

How fast? Well, in our first 5 years of discovering Direct Response, my wife Eileen and I turned our $300 investment into a total of over $10,000,000 cash! We became instant millionaires and fell madly in love with this amazing "hands-off" marketing.

We built a huge library filled from floor to ceiling with books and tapes. We attended seminars, hired all of the top consultants in this field and spent the next 25 years studying and testing every aspect of this exciting way to make money. Over the years, among many "failures" along the way, we perfected our skills and discovered all of the hidden secrets that ended up bringing us...

Over $150-Million Dollars!

So when a friend told me about a Network Marketing company that was truly innovative – I was chomping at the bit to see how our proven multi-million dollar Direct Response methods would work. I got started right away, worked our proven system and – as you already know – I brought in almost a quarter of a million dollars in my first nine weeks and am on my way to making millions...

That's When I Woke Up!

Suddenly a powerful idea hit me like a ton of bricks! You see, we've been teaching people how to get rich in Direct Response Marketing for years. So after achieving almost instant success in Network Marketing, I decided to teach all of the powerful methods we had discovered in Direct Response Marketing to all of the people who want to get rich in Network Marketing!

So now that you know a little about me, it's time to teach you a few important things about Direct Response. Please read closely.

What makes this form of marketing so special?

When done correctly, here's what this amazing marketing method can do for you:

1. Direct Response gives you a powerful way to sell to millions of people without talking to anyone!

2. This works like a powerful magnet to attract only the people you most want to attract into your Network Marketing organization. It attracts the right people and repels the wrong ones – automatically!

3. When set up correctly – a good Direct Response promotion can be "systematized" to bring in huge sums of VERY PREDICTABLE INCOME that can be generated with almost no time or work. In other words...

Once You Get the Right Campaign
Tested and Making Money on a Small Scale –
All You Have to Do is Turn Up the Volume
to Get Huge Sums of Cash Flowing to You!

This is a automatic way for you and your Distributors to build a massive downline that can make you a fortune! When set up correctly – all of the people in your organization can each do a small amount of effort that can add up to massive sums of money for them and, most importantly, for you!

This is so great that I must tell you again. Please read closely: When you have a good system that has been set up that has been tested and proven to make money – all you have to do is let your downline use it to make money for themselves and you! This is the ultimate way to combine Direct Response and Network Marketing! And...

This is the Golden Secret
That Could Easily Be Worth
Millions of Dollars to You!

Let me give you an example of how easy this can be. First, let me tell you what a good Direct Response promotion is NOT. Direct response marketing is not throwing a CD, a DVD and a flyer in an envelope and mailing it to a cold prospect. Many people falsely believe they're using Direct Response Marketing, but they're doing it all wrong – and they're getting terrible results because of it.

Good, proven Direct Response Marketing is a series of ads and sales material that attract the exact type of prospect you are searching for. It usually consists of what we call a "2-step lead generating ad" and a series of special "follow-up" sales materials. It is these ads and sales materials that do all of the selling for you and your Distributors.

1. They get the exact type of person you are looking for to "raise their hand" and prove to you that they are interested.

2. Then it does a complete job of selling that person on all of the greatest benefits of your particular Network Marketing opportunity.

3. Then it makes it super easy for these people to get started right away!

And now for the most important part: These people can all flood into your downline like a raging river.

Putting You in Position to Make a Huge On-Going Residual Income as They Use the Same Direct Response System You are Using!

Consider the power behind this amazing

marketing method:

A.   You only attract the best prospects who are most likely to become great distributors for your Network Marketing opportunity.

B.   Your sales material and complete Direct Response Marketing System do all of the actual selling for you!

C.   The only time you will actually speak to anyone (and only if and when you want!) it will be to the best people who are 100% sold and ready to help make you huge sums of money!

This gives you...

A Complete "Marketing System"
That works Like a Money Machine!

This system does all of the selling for you and your Distributors:

✔   There's no need for opportunity meetings.

✔   No endless phone calls and cold prospecting.

✔   No more headaches and hassles of dealing with losers who will never achieve any real success or people who only waste your precious time and energy.

✔   No more personal selling whatsoever!

A great Direct Response Marketing System solves most of the biggest problems in Network Marketing: The fact that...

Most People are Terrible Sales People!

You can put these people in front of the very

AUTOMATIC RECRUITING SYSTEM

best prospects and they'll screw it up every time! These people couldn't sell fast-food burgers to a starving crowd. However, here's the flip side of the coin: Many of these non-sales types are also some of the most loyal and dedicated people on the planet! In other words: If you can give these people a proven way to make money they will stay in your organization for the rest of their lives and continue bringing you huge profits for many years!

And that brings me to the second major problem. More often than not...

The best sales people make the worst Distributors!

Listen closely – I am proud to be a salesman. To me, selling is the greatest profession on earth! But there is a dark side to many salespeople. Here it is: We tend to be somewhat "flighty." We get excited very easily and are capable of doing a tremendous job of selling while we are in love with some new opportunity that has fired-up our imagination. But then we tend to lose interest just as quickly... We end up jumping from one opportunity to another. (You're nodding your head as you read this, aren't you?)

The fact is: Most Network Marketing opportunities are best suited for people who know how to sell. but most people hate selling! Can you see how crazy this is? Doesn't this explain 90% of all the failure behind most Network Marketing opportunities? You bet it does!

These People Would Rather Go to the Dentist to Have a Tooth Pulled Than to Stay Home All Day and Make One Phone Call After Another.

But personal selling is what traditional Network Marketing is all about. And those who cannot or will not sell do not last long. That's where Direct Response Marketing comes into play. This is a powerful form of selling without personal involvement.

Think about the number of items you have bought, because:

- You received a letter in the mail.

- You saw a commercial on T.V..

- You found a website on the Internet.

- You heard a commercial on the radio.

Think carefully about all of the items you own right now that were purchased because of some type of Direct Response offer. In every case – you are being "sold" without talking to anyone.

That's what Direct Response Marketing is

all about:

It's Making Huge Numbers of Sales –
Without Any Personal Selling!

When used correctly – a great Direct
Response System can sell huge numbers of
people on your Network Marketing company and
its products. This is the golden key to making
huge sums of money without talking to anyone!
It's the powerful way to get rich in Network
Marketing without any of the headaches and
hassles of personal selling. In short, it's the
hidden secret that you have been searching for to
make a huge fortune!

The famous billionaire Aristotle Onassis
once said that the secret to getting rich is simple:
"Just know something that none of your
competitors know." And if you have read this far,
you know that good Direct Response Marketing is

a secret that will give you a tremendous edge over all of the other Network Marketing Distributors who are competing against you!

Maybe you're asking yourself, "Why don't more Distributors and Network Marketing companies use this powerful form of marketing?" That's a great question for the next Chapter! Please read it now!

CHAPTER FIVE

If Direct Response Marketing is Such a Great Way to Get Rich in Network Marketing, Why Don't More People Use It?

As you saw in the last Chapter, Direct Response Marketing is a powerful way to build a huge downline – without the headaches and hassles of personal selling. Plus, I told you that the first time I used these unique methods to promote a Network Marketing opportunity...

The more you know about these little-known secrets, the more you'll have the ability to use them to become very rich!

But you may be wondering...

If Direct Response is the Ultimate Way to Become a Network Marketing Millionaire, Why Aren't More People Cashing-in with It?

This question leads to some exciting answers! Please read closely. First, let me tell you about the top 4 benefits of using the power of Direct Response Marketing to build your Network Marketing business. Here they are:

1.   This marketing method does a powerful job of selling your company's products and opportunity without any

personal rejection.

2.   It can turn good reliable distributors who hate to sell or don't want to sell into powerful salespeople!

3.   When used correctly – it is a 100% no rejection method of selling! The only time you ever speak with a single person is after you know they're 100% committed!

4.   There are many things you can do to pre-qualify prospects and let their actions tell you just how serious they are.

Direct Response Marketing is a proven way to sell a wide variety of products and services. According to the Direct Marketing Association, over 267 billion dollars worth of products and services are sold through this powerful, but highly misunderstood, form of marketing. My own company started with only $300 and quickly parlayed the profits back into more ads and direct mail letters that brought us over $10,000,000 in our first five years. Since that time, we've used these powerful methods to make over $150-million dollars in just 25 years! And many people make our fortune look pale by comparison.

So why don't more Network Markers use this powerful form of marketing? There are three main reasons:

1. The learning curve is fairly high and painful.

2. It can take a long time to 'master' this form of marketing.

3. People make half-hearted attempts, don't get the instant results they want

and give up.

Let's cover the last item first. This helps explain the first two items on our list. Please read closely, because –

If You Get a Good Understanding
of Everything in This Book –
You Can Make a Fortune!

Many people dream about getting rich in mail-order and on the Internet. But most go into this game without knowing the rules. These Direct Response Marketing newbies get very excited in the beginning. Then they experience a few minor set-backs and quit. We run into people all the time who say: "Oh, I tried to make money in mail-order (or on the Internet) and it didn't work!" Well it does work! Many people all across America are quietly depositing millions into their bank accounts with this powerful form of marketing!

But, the results you get from your first attempts are usually not very encouraging. Why? Well, that brings us to the first two items on our list.

Direct-Response Takes a Day to
Learn and a Lifetime to Master.

The most successful Direct Response Marketers have been in business for at least a decade or two. Does that discourage you? If shouldn't. After all, most Network Marketing millionaires have been in this industry for a decade or two. In fact, ALL of the worlds richest people have consistently paid the largest price for the longest period of time. Why should this be any different? If you can't accept the fact that there is a major price to pay to master the skills of making millions of dollars in any method, you will not get rich.

ARE YOU WILLING?

Listen closely, all of the ads make it seem

like they have a simple way to make money. However, those who get rich in Network Marketing have taken the time to master all of the fundamentals and the more advanced methods. This is also the 'secret' to getting rich with Direct Response Marketing. If you are willing to learn and apply your knowledge, I can teach you how to become a 'mailbox millionaire' within the next few years! Are you willing to put in some time and effort to learn and master these secrets? If so, I'll work with you and help you use the power of Direct Response Marketing to build a huge downline that can make you super rich! Best of all, you'll make all of this money without any of the headaches that other distributors are going through right now.

WHY PEOPLE FAIL IN D.R.M..

Many distributors fail because they think that mailing their company's DVDs, catalogs and other promotional materials will automatically make people want to join their group. Nothing could be further from the truth! In fact, here are 3-things you must know about this marketing method:

FACT #1: Good Direct Response Marketing is NOT about renting mailing lists of Network Marketing junkies and sending postcards or sales letters to them.

FACT #2: You can't make money by throwing a bunch of your company's booklets, DVDs, or sample products into an envelope and mailing it.

FACT #3: The right D.R.M. Campaign can make you more money than most doctors and lawyers can only dream of making!

A good Direct Response campaign is targeted and seductive. It attracts the right kind of people you are looking for and leads them through the entire buying process. Throwing your company's promotional materials in an envelope and mailing them to new prospects is a costly and stupid way to use this powerful form of marketing. However, the same sales materials that your company has developed to be handed out to the prospects can and should be used in your Direct Response Marketing System. But you must do it the right way. That's one of the things we'll talk about in the next Chapter.

WHAT TO EXPECT IN THE NEXT CHAPTER.

In the final Chapter of this Section, I'm going to give you a great analogy to help you understand this multi-billion dollar Direct Response Marketing method: DATING! I'll tell you a story about one of my millionaire friends who used his Direct

Response Marketing skills to meet some very beautiful women. You'll see what he did right and wrong. You're going to love this story! After all, one of the most powerful things about Direct Response Marketing is that it lets you instantly attract the exact type of person you are looking for. – But you must be careful! There's a powerful lesson here that could be worth a fortune to you!

But that's not all! I'm also going to give you some wisdom from one of the greatest American presidents, Abraham Lincoln. You'll discover what this unique man knew about influencing large groups of people, that can help you establish your perfect game plan for making millions of dollars! So please think carefully about the things you have already learned in the last Chapter. Then continue reading carefully and I'll show you how to begin using your new knowledge to make all of the money you want, need and truly deserve!

CHAPTER SIX

What Did Abraham Lincoln Say That Can Help You Get Rich?

If you've been reading along for the last two Chapters, you know: my job is to show you how to use the awesome power of Direct Response Marketing to build a huge Network Marketing downline – without the headaches of personal selling and recruiting.

So let's pick up where we left off in the last Chapter. Read closely and I'll give you a couple of great analogies to help you understand a few of the basic secrets for getting rich with this highly misunderstood form of marketing.

The first one is...

"DATING."

Consider this: No single guy would walk up to a beautiful woman and say "Would you go to bed with me?" She'll throw a drink in his face or slap him! The only woman who would say "YES! LET'S GO, NOW!!" is either mentally deranged, a prostitute, or coyote-ugly!

This reminds me of a millionaire friend of ours who wanted to meet some of the most beautiful women in his city. So he wrote an ad to place in the "singles" section of his local newspaper that read: "Millionaire businessman seeks fun-loving attractive woman for great times." And then he added...

"I Give Great Weekend Vacations!"

He showed the ad to me before he ran it. "Any suggestions?" he asked. "Yes!" I shouted! "Don't you dare run this! If you do, every ruthless gold-digger within 100 miles will call you! And some of these women might hit you in the head and run off with your wallet – or worse! They may seduce you into a quick marriage and then get a divorce attorney to steal half of your fortune!"

Can you see the mistake he almost made?

OKAY, here's the lesson: The most powerful thing about Direct Response Marketing is the fact that it lets you instantly attract the exact type of person you are looking for. But you must be careful! You must have a very clear idea of who you want to attract and what to say to gain their attention and interest. In other words, you can't go out there 'half-cocked' with some hazy idea and expect to make a ton of money. You must put some time and thought into your overall strategy.

Here's the second analogy: It's a quote from one of America's greatest presidents...

"If I had 3 hours to chop down a big tree –
I'd spend the first two hours sharpening my axe!"
Abraham Lincoln (a leader who knew
how to influence large groups of people)!

Abe was right! You'd be stupid to chop down a big tree with a dull axe. And yet, this is the way thousands of people approach Direct Response Marketing. These ambitious newbies have no real game plan. – For example, they cannot answer these basic questions:

1.   Who are you trying to reach?

2.   What separates what you offer from all

the rest of the people who are trying to reach and influence that same person?

3.   How is your product, service or opportunity better than all the competitors?

Why can't most Network Marketers answer these 3 basic questions? That's simple.

There's Nothing Unique
About What They Offer.

There is nothing unique about most Distributors that makes other people want to sign up in their group. Is this your problem? If so, don't be discouraged. Because I'll show you how to create your own "unique opportunity within your opportunity." You'll discover how simple it can be to create something new within your Network Marketing Opportunity that separates

YOU from all the other Distributors.

Do you see the importance of this 'axe sharpening' analogy? Good!

Please listen carefully. One of the greatest success principals is to "know exactly what you want." The clearer your vision of what you want, the more powerful your plan will be to get it. This is true in all aspects of life and business. It's especially true in Direct Response Marketing. Here's how: The more specific you are about the exact type of person you're searching for – the better you will be at developing a powerful and effective Marketing System to attract huge numbers of these people. Sounds like common sense? Well, as Mark Twain once said: "Common sense is a very uncommon thing." He was right!

These ideas are very simple. In fact, they're too simple for most people. They will never take

the time to use this "axe sharpening secret."
They will never ask themselves the 3 very basic
questions above. And because of that – they will
always fail to get the results they want. Their axe
is dull and the tree is thick! They will take their
dull axe and begin chopping away with all their
strength and...

They'll Wear Out Fast and Give Up
or Die of a Heart Attack!

The smart person takes the Abraham Lincoln
analogy one step further: Instead of sharpening
their axe – they go out and buy the biggest and
most powerful chainsaw they can find! Then, in
the time it takes to sharpen an axe – they have
chopped down many trees and turned them into
a truckload of firewood!

Here's the lesson: Trying to attract hundreds
or thousands of the exact type of person you're

searching for – and offering them something that is truly different – is as difficult as cutting down dozens of giant trees for your winter supply of firewood. This is not easy! However, if your chainsaw is powerful enough – you can do the job quickly and have enough firewood left over to sell to many other people!

Anyway, I wanted you to have these two analogies to try to help you understand the power of a great Direct Response Marketing System. You see, once you set this System up the right way, you can do something that most Network Marketers will never be able to do:

This Marketing System can quickly
go to work for you to bring you
hundreds or even thousands of
the exact type of people you are
searching for to build your downline!

Do it right and you can use this powerful

form of marketing to make huge sums of money by only attracting the people who will end up becoming your very best distributors and make you the largest amount of money!

Does all this sound too good to be true? It's not! In fact, we are getting ready to launch a whole new kind of Network Marketing company that lets you use the awesome power of Direct-Response Marketing to make GIANT sums of money!

Best of all, you can make ALL of this money – without talking to a single person!

Are you interested?

You should be. Especially if you went over this Section!

So please go on to the final Section. I can't wait to tell you about our proven opportunity that lets you use the awesome power of Direct Response Marketing to get rich in Network Marketing! Please read this Section now and follow the instructions to get started at once!

SECTION THREE

Our 3-Step System and the Proven Passive Income System That Lets You Make Money by Helping Other People!

In this Section I will give you all of the secrets behind our 3-Step Automatic Recruiting System. Then, in the final Chapter, I will tell you about our Easy Passive Income System. Remember, this is not a traditional Network Marketing opportunity, but it does pay on several levels and has many advantages that could potentially add up to huge sums of money for you.

CHAPTER SEVEN

The Three Easy Steps and Why They Work.

This Chapter gives you a summary of the promises I made to promote this book. With these secrets, you can make money in any network or affiliate marketing program with no personal selling.

Let's start with the 3 steps to our Automatic Recruiting System:

1.   Create a series of information products that sell people on the benefits of working with you and

getting involved in your opportunity and your complete Marketing System that makes it easy to get started and make money.

2.   Use our Direct Response Marketing Methods to create and then offer your system that attracts people into your team.

3.   Let the people in your sales organization use your Marketing System to duplicate your results.

That's it. Just 3 simple steps. Write them down. Refer back to them often. As you can see, each one is clear and simple. But don't let the simplicity fool you. These are the same steps that have brought me tens of millions of dollars. They are the same steps used by successful Network Marketing distributors who have learned how to combine the power of Direct Response Marketing with Network Marketing. Now you can join them!

So, with that in mind, let's go over the promises I made in the advertisements to promote this book. Read carefully. By the time you're finished, you'll know exactly how the 3-step system above could make you set for life.

How to Get People Standing in Line and
Beg You to Let Them Join Your Team!

The first step in our system is creating a series of information products. An information product is the perfect way to attract the right kind of people to you because...

- It proves you are an expert. It lets the right prospects know that you have the knowledge they're looking for. People love working with experts who can help them get more of what they want the most.

- It lets you attract the right people. You only attract the best people who are searching for what you offer, which is a better way to make money in Network Marketing. Your information products show these people that you have a way to give them all the major benefits that a Network Marketing opportunity has, without the hassles of traditional recruiting methods.

- It doesn't matter what format you use. It could be a book like this one, a video series, an audio program, or a blog. The format doesn't matter. What does matter is that you're separating yourself from other distributors who are using traditional

Network Marketing recruiting methods. When you use our system the right way, you'll have people practically begging to be a part of your team.

How to Make Massive Money at Lightning Speed.

The second step in our system is designed to make you super-fast cash by offering your advertising and marketing services to the people who purchase your information products.

This is how it works: Your complete Marketing System will include advertising and marketing services that are built around your information products. The sale of your marketing services is great for your team of distributors, because it gives them the same automated system you're using to make money. Offering advertising and marketing services to the people on your team gives you the fast cash you need right now.

How to Use 100% FREE ADVERTISING
to Recruit Large Numbers of People.

Your information products become part of your proprietary Marketing System that ALL of the people on your team can use to build their own sales organization. They use your system to promote your information products to attract people to their team. This lets them spend their money while ultimately helping you build your sales team.

Here's how it works: You allow all the people on your team to use your Marketing System to build their business. This is brilliant because of how Network Marketing is designed to pay commissions for building your team. The more they do to build their income, the more money

they ultimately make for you! While your
distributors are spending their own money to build
their teams, they are actively promoting you and
your system. They're building a solid business and
you're cashing in on 100% FREE ADVERTISING.

How to Find the Best People Who Can
Make You an Endless Stream of Big Money.

One of the biggest lies that all Network
Marketing companies tell you is that everyone you
come in contact with could become a great
distributor in your organization. This is wrong in
so many ways. Just because anyone can do this
business doesn't mean they will. In fact, very few
will. Your Marketing System must be designed to
attract people who will most likely become your
best distributors. These people are few and far
between. After all, most people think Network
Marketing is nothing but a scam. The majority will
always be completely turned off by it and there's

nothing you can do to change their minds. That's why your Marketing System should be designed to only seek out people who have previous experience in this business.

How to Separate Yourself from 99%
of Network or Affiliate Marketers.

Most network marketers do no marketing. That may sound funny, but it's true! You see, good marketing is all the things that you do to separate yourself from everyone else. And most network marketers are using the same ineffective recruiting methods that everyone else is using. You can't make this mistake. And now you won't!

A good Marketing System separates you from everyone else. There must be something unique about you and what you offer to make it compelling enough for the best prospects to seek you out and join your team. That's what our 3-

step system does this for you.

Millions of people desperately want and need to make more money. Many of them have been exposed to at least one Network Marketing opportunity in the past. They like some of the benefits of this business, such as residual income, being part of a team and making money by helping other people. But they HATE all the recruiting methods that force them to bother their friends and family members. Your Marketing System shows these people how they can get all the benefits this business has to offer – without the headaches and hassles. This instantly separates you from 99% of the other network marketers and makes the best people want to join your team.

How Our Complete Marketing System Gives You an Unfair Advantage Over Everyone Else.

The Greek shipping billionaire Aristotle

AUTOMATIC RECRUITING SYSTEM

Onassis once said that "the secret to business is to know something none of your competitors knows." That one idea brought him billions of dollars. Now his secret can make YOU massive sums of money! Here's how: Our system is built around Direct Response Marketing. This is something most network marketers and the companies they promote know nothing about. This form of marketing generates billions of dollars every year. It eliminates the need for personal selling. The only people you talk to are those who are already 100% pre-sold and ready to join. This gives you a genuine unfair advantage over all the other network marketers you're competing with.

How to Be a Top Distributor in Any Company.

Millions of people would love to get paid the huge residual incomes that Network Marketing opportunities provide, but...

✔   They don't want to sell...

✔   They don't want to bother their friends and family...

✔   And they hate going to opportunity meetings and Network Marketing pep rallies.

If only these people could make huge sums of residual income without all these headaches and hassles, wouldn't that be great? WELL NOW THEY CAN! You'll be helping them do it when you use our 3-step Automatic Recruiting System. This gives you the power to be a top distributor in any company.

How the 3rd Step Creates a Huge Team of Distributors Working for You.

Letting the people in your sales organization

use your Automatic Recruiting System can cause your downline to explode! Millions want and need more money and that's exactly what your Marketing System does for them. There are millions of people already involved in a Network Marketing opportunity and many of these people are tired of the traditional recruiting methods and are looking for an easier and better system to make money. When you help these people do this, you'll cause your own organization to explode with growth!

How to Build Your Income
with the Magic of Timing.

People love to buy but hate to be sold. They hate to be high-pressured. Unfortunately, all the traditional Network Marketing recruiting methods force you to do the high pressure selling (even when they say they don't). With traditional methods, you are approaching the wrong people who would never even consider joining a Network

Marketing opportunity. With our Automatic Recruiting System, you are only attracting the people who have already proven that they are interested. You're catching the right people at the right time and presenting your offer to them in the right way. This takes the pressure off them. They feel it's their decision. And because of these things, they're much more open and receptive to checking out everything you have to offer and (hopefully) quickly joining your team.

How to Build Unbreakable Bonds
of Loyalty Within Your Team.

Giving people a way to make money in Network Marketing without all the headaches and hassles will bond them to you. Your system gives them solutions they can't get anywhere else. Remember, traditional recruiting is hard. It forces most people to do things they're not comfortable doing. Most people hate all of this, but don't know there's a better way. Everybody's just following each other down the same road of desperation and frustration.

With traditional recruiting methods, there's nothing to separate you from anyone else. There's no reason for anyone to choose to sign up under you. If you're using these traditional recruiting methods right now, you must break out of this rut. That's what you're doing when you use our system: you are creating your own proprietary informational products that the people on your team will spend their own time and money to promote. Plus, your Direct Response Marketing System makes sales, with no personal selling! Your distributors on your team will never want to quit when they're using your system and getting results.

How to Find Thousands of Eager People
Who Quickly Join Your Team.

Your Automatic Recruiting System searches

for the right people who are searching for you. This attracts the best prospects who prove they are serious about finding a better way to make money in Network Marketing. With the standard methods of recruiting, there is no way to find and attract thousands of eager people. You're taught that all you have to do is recruit a handful of people who will also recruit a handful of others, etc. Supposedly, this will lead to thousands of distributors in your organization. That never happens. In fact, it's one of the biggest Network Marketing lies. After all, the people who are making the largest amount of money are the heavy hitters who have systems for attracting hundreds or thousands of distributors from their efforts alone.

THE BOTTOM LINE: You can't win when you follow traditional recruiting methods, because you're never able to recruit enough people fast enough. Our Automatic Recruiting System is different. It uses your information products and

Direct Response Marketing to attract the best people. This gives you the power to be a heavy hitter and attract thousands of people who are eager to join your team.

How to Avoid the Dirty Dark Secret
That Causes Many Distributors to Fail.

Network Marketing distributors unknowingly lie by repeating the company line that all you have to do is introduce a few people to the opportunity who also do the same. They teach you that you can ultimately build a large organization through every person on your team who each does a small amount of recruiting. So for example, if you have 5 distributors who go out and recruit 5 more and that's duplicated a few more times, you'll ultimately have thousands of distributors in your organization.

In theory, here's what it looks like to build a

team this way:

$$5 \times 5 = 25$$

$$25 \times 5 = 125$$

$$125 \times 5 = 625$$

$$625 \times 5 = 3,125$$

$$3,125 \times 5 = 15,625$$

All that sounds great. But don't believe it for a minute. It may work on paper, but it doesn't work that way in the real world. In fact, it never happens. Instead, you need to do what the heavy hitters do: Use a system to quickly bring in hundreds of people into your organization. Then teach them to use your system to do the same. That's what all 3 steps in our system are designed to do for you.

AUTOMATIC RECRUITING SYSTEM

Why Most Recruiting Methods
are Wasteful and Stupid.

Making a list of your friends and family and all the people you've ever known and then approaching them about your network or affiliate marketing opportunity is the dumbest thing you can do. No wonder most people don't make it in this business. This is ridiculous. It's beyond stupid. As you probably already know, most of your friends and acquaintances have no interest in your Network Marketing opportunity, no matter how fantastic it is. This business model only appeals to a certain kind of person.

But our system solves this problem. The advertising you'll use goes out into the market and searches for the people who have already been exposed to Network Marketing. The advertising attracts people who are looking for a faster, easier and simpler way to make money in Network Marketing. Anything that doesn't seek to attract this type of perfect prospect into your organization is not only wasteful, but it's insulting to the people who have no interest in this business.

Two Reasons Why "Heavy Hitters" are Bad for Your Team.

Most people in Network Marketing have been taught that all they need to do is recruit one heavy hitter and they'll be set for life. They believe they can sit back and watch this heavy hitter sign up hundreds of people into their team and then they'll be set for life. Of course, it never works that way. Even if you do recruit a superstar and they do bring you a lot of people, they can leave anytime and take most of your team with them. Plus, these people tend to be very demanding. They can drive you crazy! So don't believe this lie. With our system, you don't need heavy-hitters. You can recruit hundreds or even thousands of people into your team without attracting a single heavy-hitter.

AUTOMATIC RECRUITING SYSTEM

Why Unhappy, Angry, Frustrated, and Miserable People Will Often Be Your Best Distributors.

A majority of the people who are searching for a business opportunity are not happy. They are angry and frustrated with their current financial situation. Their money problems make them downright miserable. And yet, their misery is what causes them to search for the solution you offer. You will be giving them a proven way to make money without all of the problems that other Network Marketing Distributors go through. Once these people begin to use your system to make money, they'll become loyal distributors who will never leave. You'll be helping them find a solution to their pain and they will reward you with their loyalty.

How to Recruit Thousands of the
Best Distributors in the Next 18 Months.

The average Network Marketing distributor only recruits two other people. Because of this, signing up dozens, let alone thousands, of distributors is virtually impossible. But as you know, the superstars in this industry achieve these kinds of results! And now, with our Automatic Recruiting System, you can have the power to do this! This system is designed to attract the very best distributors. Then those people will also use your system to achieve the same results. This has a snowball effect as you and all the members of your team continue to use this system to attract a large and growing number of new distributors. Although there are no guarantees, within 18 months your team could explode with growth and provide you with huge monthly profits!

The 3 BIGGEST LIES That Network Marketing Companies Tell You.

Many companies lie, steal and cheat their distributors. They make even the dirtiest politicians look like angels. You can suffer greatly if you fall for their lies.

Here are the 3 BIGGEST LIES:

LIE #1.   All you have to do is just recruit a few people.

The companies try to convince you that all you have to do is sign up a handful of people. They tell you this will make you massive sums of money when those people and others in your group do the same. But this never happens. It's a lie and they know it. All you have to do is look at the people who are making the largest sum of money and you'll see: they are always the heavy hitters who are capable of bringing in hundreds or thousands of distributors on their own.

LIE #2.   You don't have to sell.

The companies tell you that introducing their

products and services isn't really "selling." Instead, they say that all you're doing is "sharing the good news" the same way you would tell a friend about a movie you wanted them to see. This is a lie and you know it, because every time you tell someone about the products and opportunity, you're really trying to convince them to join your sales team. You know it. The company knows it. What's worse, your friends know it, too!

LIE #3. You can get rich.

The companies want you to believe that you can get rich using their traditional recruiting methods. But it's not true. Remember, most people never make any real money in Network Marketing. It is true that all the top companies have distributors who are making high six- and seven-figure annual incomes. But these people are not your "Average Joe." They're high-powered, charismatic sales people who have spent a lifetime developing the qualities that have taken them to the top. Few people have the desire or the time to develop these skills.

So don't fall for any of these 3 lies. With our system, you'll have the ability to cash-in big by signing up hundreds or even thousands of people without doing any traditional recruiting.

Why the Standard Sales Materials
the Network Marketing Companies
Provide to You are Worthless.

All Network Marketing companies use what we call "image-based advertising." This simply means no special offer is being made and there's no compelling reason for your prospects to take action. This is like most of the commercials you see on TV for huge companies like McDonald's and Coke. This kind of advertising may work for those giant multinational corporations, but it does a lousy job of recruiting them into your team.

So, if the advertising they give you doesn't sell, what does?

You know the answer: IT'S YOU!

But our methods are different. The turn-key system you'll be using is based on our proven Direct Response Marketing methods. These methods have generated tens of millions of dollars for us. Now, we're teaching you everything we know. This form of marketing does all the selling for you. You don't have to personally sell anything. The only people you'll speak to will be pre-sold ~ super excited~ and ready to get started!

How to Get RICH by Giving People
Something They Can't Get Anywhere Else.

Most people hate traditional recruiting

methods. They don't want to bother their friends and family. They hate 3-way calls and the 3-Foot Rule! They can't stand the pep rallies and opportunity meetings.

Can you relate to this? Do you hate all the things you have to go through to build your sales organization? If so, you'll love the fact that our methods let you make money in any Network Marketing company without these headaches and hassles. Best of all, you'll be offering this same advantage to the huge market of millions of people who are searching for a simple, easy and proven way to make money. This kind of automated Marketing System gives them something they can't get anywhere else.

The Proven Marketing System That
Can Bring You Thousands of Distributors.

My wife and I became multi-millionaires in a

few short years thanks to Direct Response Marketing. Now we've taken the best of the best of all of our powerful secrets that we've used to generate millions of dollars and built them into this powerful time-tested system.

With these methods, it doesn't matter where you live. Our company is headquartered in a small town in the middle of Kansas and yet we've used these marketing methods to do business with over one million people. Think about that. Here we are, doing business all over the world from a small town. And yet, we've used our Marketing System to get in front of tens of millions of prospects. Think of the power this can give you!

How Step 3 Gives You the Power
to Become a Multi-Millionaire.

With the third step, you are letting the people in your sales organization cash in with the same system that sold them. Remember, tens of millions of people are searching for the best way to make money. They're looking for a proven method that will let them make the largest amount of money, in the shortest period of time, with the least amount of work. That's what our system is designed to do. Best of all, having hundreds or even thousands of distributors using your Marketing System to build their team could ultimately bring you up to millions of dollars, just as it has for us.

How to Build an Iron Cage
Around the People in Your Group.

Once somebody starts using your Marketing System and getting results, they'll never want to stop. This creates a tremendous amount of loyalty within your organization. You can think of it as an iron cage that will keep them locked into your sales organization forever! Now other network marketers can't steal them away from you.

How to Make the Kind of Money Most
Doctors and Lawyers Only Dream of.

Step 1 of our system lets you brand yourself.
With this Step, you are creating a series of
information products that promote you and your
organization. This makes you an expert and
draws people to you. Everyone wants to do
business with someone who has established
themselves as an authority. That's the position
you'll put yourself in when you use Step 1. Best of
all, when you join our team, you'll cash in with all
of the information products that we have already
developed for you. As you'll see in the next
Chapter, this has the potential to pay you huge
sums of money in just minutes a day!

How to Find Millions of Hot Prospects
Who are Eager to Join Your Group.

With our system, you're not confined to

recruiting in your own area. The world is your marketplace. All the advertising that you and the people in your sales organization do will reach out to the huge worldwide market of people who are searching for the best way to make money! There's never been a more exciting time to use our methods. For example, Facebook alone has over one billion members. That's potentially millions of hot prospects through just one website alone. Think of the power this gives you and all the people on your team!

An Ethical Way to "Steal" the Best Distributors From Other Top Performers.

The best prospective distributors for your organization have already been sold on the benefits of Network Marketing. These are the only kind of people who understand all the problems with traditional recruiting methods. Because of that, they will truly appreciate and understand the benefits that your AUTOMATIC MARKETING SYSTEM provides to them.

There are over 15 million active Network Marketing distributors in the USA alone. And for every one of these people, there are probably another ten who have been exposed to this business. That's tens of millions of hot prospects who don't have to be sold on the potential power of Network Marketing or the benefits of using your automated system.

The advertising that you and your distributors do will reach out to this huge market and show them how they can get all the benefits of a Network Marketing business without all the headaches and hassles they're going through now. You become the solution they're looking for. This is an ethical way to pull them away from the other organizations they're already a part of – and bring them into your team.

AUTOMATIC RECRUITING SYSTEM

The Hidden Secret That Most Successful Network Marketers Use to Make $50,000 to $100,000 a Month.

These Network Marketing superstars have achieved celebrity status. They may not be known to the average person, but in Network Marketing circles, they've become famous! Because of that fame, they're able to move from company to company and take their loyal fans with them. That's the power of a heavy hitter. And that's the same type of power you'll have with our proven 3-Step System.

How to Tap into "Virgin Markets" of Sane, Stable and Committed Distributors Other Network Marketers are Not Able to Recruit.

In addition to active network marketers, our system has the power to also attract people who have no Network Marketing experience. They have never been tainted. They're good, average, sane, stable people who are searching for a simple and easy part-time business. They're looking for a way to put in a few hours a week and replace their full-time income. When these people see the benefits you provide, they'll quickly join your team and become the kind of loyal distributors who can make you money for years.

How Some Network Marketers are Already Using Step 1 to Make $50,000 a Month or More.

Most distributors are all the same. Because of this, there is no compelling reason for others to join their team. They're afraid to do anything to draw attention to themselves and their opportunity. You can't make this mistake. Remember, the most successful distributors do a really good job of branding and promoting themselves. They do things to bond people to them. They tell their story. They promote themselves. They build empathy. All of these things endear people to them and allow them to build huge teams and earn massive sums of money. As you know, these are the things our system will do for you.

How to Attract Thousands of New Distributors by Solving Their Biggest Problem.

People want to make a lot of money. But they don't want to go through the headaches and hassles of starting and running a business. The most successful person I've ever met told me something I'll never forget. He said, "What people really want is a money machine. This gives them all of the benefits of a business, without the pain." That's what your Marketing System is designed to do for them. It can solve the biggest problem they have and draw thousands of people to you.

How to Get Rich From the "MLM Junkies" and Other "Losers" that Most Network Marketers Avoid.

Millions of people have been around the

Network Marketing industry for decades. Many of these people have joined dozens of companies. They get involved in a new Network Marketing opportunity and get really excited. When they fail to make money fast enough, they drop out and move on to the next company. A percentage of these people have been involved in dozens of network and affiliate marketing opportunities. We affectionately call them "MLM Junkies." Many established network marketers avoid these people and think of them as losers, because they never stick with any of the opportunities they join. They don't even try to sign these types of people up. Yet, these people can become your very best distributors because when you give them the right system, they can make money for the first time in their lives. And once you help them make money, they'll stay with you and never leave.

How Step 2 Makes People Want to Join Your Team.

You must reach the right people at the right

AUTOMATIC RECRUITING SYSTEM

time and sell them the way they want to be sold.
Your prospect must feel it is their decision to buy.
Your automated system does a good job of "soft-
selling" people. You can use autoresponders and
other methods to stay in close touch with your
prospects and continue to build a strong
relationship with them. Over a period of time, this
makes them want to join your team. Each follow-
up email, letter, webinar, or tele-seminar cranks up
the volume on their emotional hot buttons and
makes them want to be part of your team.
Throughout this entire process, you're making
them feel more like it's their decision to get
involved and use your system.

How a Few People Stumbled Upon
Step 1 and are Now Set for Life.

Some network marketers have developed
their own systems for making fast and easy money.
They've passed them on to their key people and

ultimately built huge sales organizations that made them financially set for life. Now they never have to worry about money ever again.

But, for every one of these people there are thousands of network marketers who have no system for making any real money. These people are using traditional recruiting methods that involve a great deal of personal selling, opportunity meetings, 3-way calls, etc. As you've seen, all of those things lead to failure. You can't waste your time with these ineffective methods. And now you won't have to!

The Secret that Millionaire Marketers Use to Get People to Stand in Line with Money in Hand.

A good automated Marketing System that's built around a solid Network Marketing company is very similar to a franchise opportunity.

Every good franchise has 3 key components:

AUTOMATIC RECRUITING SYSTEM

1.   A product or service that's a proven seller.

2.   A system to attract and retain customers.

3.   Help, support and guidance from experts who understand the business.

Those 3 ingredients are responsible for the one trillion dollars that are generated each year by the franchise industry. Best of all, these are the same ingredients you'll have with our Automatic Recruiting System. When people see the benefits your system provides, they will practically stand in line with money in hand!

The "Hot Button Secret" in Step 2 That Pays You Maximum Money in Minimum Time.

With our system, you will find the best people who are searching for you. These are the people who desperately want and need the benefits you offer. Your automated Marketing System is designed to prove that you have the solutions they seek. The synergy of hundreds or even thousands of people in your sales organization who are using your system can pay you huge sums of money very quickly. Then it quickly signs them up and cash-in with the same system you're using.

How to Guarantee Your People
Will Never Drop Out.

People drop out of your team because they're not making enough money fast enough. Plus, they hate all the headaches and hassles they have to go through with traditional recruiting methods. But with Step 3, you're letting them use your automated Marketing System that makes it easy for them to make money. Once they do start making money, they'll never want to stop. You'll have provided the solution to their problems and they will thank you for it with their loyalty.

How Step 2 Finds Thousands of Eager Prospects Who Can't Wait to Join Your Team.

Millions of people are searching for the benefits a good home business opportunity provides. For example, look at the baby boomer marketplace alone. There is an estimated 76 million people in the United States who were born between 1946 and 1964. The first people in this group began retiring as early as 2007 – 2008. Many of these people are finding that they need more money or they're looking for the excitement of a part-time home business. You're system attracts these people and gives them the benefit they're searching for. Your system attracts these people and gives them the benefit they're searching for. It draws them to you and promises them the solution they're searching for. Then, it compels them to take an initial action, which proves they are serious.

How Our System Gets the Best People to Prove They're Interested.

Everyone "says" they want to make more money. But most people are not serious. They may dream about making more money, but they're unwilling to actually do anything about it. The steps in our proven system work like magic to attract the best people to you. The actions they take (such as attending a Webinar, a Tele-Seminar, or sending for a Free Report or DVD, requesting a copy of your eBook, etc.) prove they are interested.

How Our System Gets People to Sign Up Under You.

The people who respond to your advertising prove they're serious. As my Grandma Clara used to say: "The only way you can tell about a person is by the actions they take." That's especially true for the people who respond to your advertising. Anyone who responds to your advertising is telling you a lot about their interest in finding the right opportunity, because they took the specific action you requested. Now you can develop a wide variety of materials that build so much value, it makes it irresistible for the right people to join your team.

How to Make it Super Easy for Your New Prospect to Get Started and Make Money.

Once people see how easy it is to use your system to make their dreams come true, they'll be eager to start. Remember, they make money using the same system that you used to attract them. This is so important! They can see how others will love using the system because they already love using it! Once they see how your Marketing System eliminates all the problems of traditional recruiting methods for them, they'll be eager to share your system with others!

How Our System Separates You from the Average Network Marketer.

To a new prospect who is looking for a way to make extra money, there's no difference between one distributor and another. There's nothing uniquely different that makes one distributor stand out. And if you're making this mistake, there's nothing to make your prospects chose you over any other network marketer.

So many people are afraid to promote themselves and do things to stand out and get noticed. This is another mistake you can't afford to make. You must develop a Marketing System that promotes you, your company and the opportunity you sell. You have to tell your story. The information products you'll develop when you use Step 1 of our system will do a great job of separating you from every other network marketer who is promoting their products and services to the same marketplace. This attracts the best people to you.

How to "Pyramid" Your Tiny Little Profits into a Huge Fortune.

This simple secret took us from humble beginnings of $300 to sales of almost $100,000 a week in no time flat. Others have used it to bring in billions. Now you can use this little-known method to fill your team with thousands of people who can make you huge sums of money for the rest of your life. Here's the secret: all you do is put a percentage of every dollar you earn back into more of the advertising and marketing that brought it to you in the first place. Do this and teach all the people in your sales organization to do the same thing and you'll "pyramid" your profits into a huge fortune.

How to Make Your Fortune by Giving People Something of Value They Can't Get Anywhere Else.

Here's my greatest secret for getting rich in two words: "IMPACT MILLIONS!" To make tremendous sums of money, you must search for something that can make a huge difference in the lives of millions of people. When you do that, you can potentially make a huge fortune! Our 3-step Marketing System is designed to help you do exactly that.

Remember this two-word formula for making a fortune. This is the real secret of success. All you are doing is finding a way to make a huge difference in the lives of people and you will get rich.

Here's the formula:

- Millions of people want to make more money.

- But they don't want to go through the nightmare of starting and running their own business.

- And when it comes to Network Marketing, they absolutely hate the traditional recruiting methods. In fact, they'd rather sit in a dentist's chair and have several teeth pulled than spend that time selling a prospect. But with our system, you are helping to give them all of the benefits of a thriving, prosperous business, without the headaches and hassles. This is the one thing that tens of millions of people who normally would not get involved in Network Marketing want the most.

Why Most Network Marketing Companies
are "Clueless" About What it Takes for
the Average Distributor to Get Rich.

Network Marketing companies know that
the few distributors within their opportunity who
are making a six- and seven- figure annual income
are extremely charismatic salespeople. These
people know how sign up thousands of people by
building automatic Marketing Systems (like the
one we're teaching you) or filling up hotel
ballrooms. Network Marketing companies know
that the traditional recruiting methods they teach
don't work for most people. They know that the
average distributor only recruits 2 other people
into their organization. Even so, they continue to
convince people that it's possible for each
distributor to sign up a few people and get rich.
They're clueless about all of the tricks and
strategies in our system that let the average
distributor make the kind of money only heavy

hitters dream of.

The Evil Secret Behind Every Network Marketing Company.

Every network and affiliate marketing company knows that an extremely large percentage of everyone who signs up will do virtually nothing and drop out within months. These people will spend good money to purchase an initial Start-Up Package. They'll purchase and use the products for a while, and may even talk to a few friends and family members before they drop out. But, they know that only a small percentage of their distributors ever make any money. Yet they continue to tell all their distributors that it's possible to make a huge 6-figure income, when industry data suggests that the average Network Marketing distributor will only earn between $500 and $2,000 a year using these traditional recruiting methods. They have no solution to offer the average distributor to help them do what they've promised can be done. With our system, you will be using proven Direct Response Marketing methods to draw people to you and help them become truly successful.

How Our System Lets Thousands of People Who Hate Network Marketing Become Your Very Best Distributors.

Tens of millions of people have been exposed to Network Marketing. Some of those people have been involved in one or two of these types of opportunities. Many others have watched their friends and family members get involved in these opportunities, get their hopes up, and then fail. All of this has led to a huge and growing number of people who hate Network Marketing. When these people see that you have a system that will allow them to attract other distributors with no personal selling and then quickly and easily help them do the same, they will take notice.

What these people really hate is not Network Marketing, it's the traditional recruiting methods that are being promoted by these companies. They realize that there's a tremendous amount of money to be made in this business. They've heard the stories of others who have started with virtually nothing and gone on to make high six- and seven-figure annual incomes. Your system is designed to attract these people by showing them how they can build a substantial income in any Network Marketing company without the headaches and hassles of traditional Network Marketing. Once they see that, they'll join your team and become loyal distributors who make you money for years.

So with all this said, now go on to the next chapter and let me tell you about the revolutionary home based business opportunity we have built our automated system around. You'll see: this is not a traditional Network Marketing opportunity. However, it does pay on several levels. And best of all, it gives you (and the people we can sign up under you) our exciting new way to make money by helping other people! Read the next Chapter for all of the details. Then fill out the last page in this book and get started at once.

CHAPTER EIGHT

Let Us Help You!

Congratulations for having officially read "Automatic Recruiting System" from beginning to end. I hope you're excited about this!

Throughout this book, I've mentioned a little about our Easy Passive Income System. This unique program contains the best of the best of Network and Direct Response Marketing. As I told you in the last Chapter, this is NOT a traditional Network Marketing opportunity. However, it does pay on several levels. And it does let you cash-in with the greatest tips, tricks, and little-known strategies we've used to bring in tens of millions of dollars.

So please read this Chapter carefully. It gives you a complete summary of our Easy Passive Income System. Discover how this is designed to pay you a potential but not promised income of up to many thousands of dollars in purely passive income. Then, fill out the Form on the last page. Do this and I will have my staff rush you the complete information package that tells you more about this amazing system and invites you to become a Representative.

With all this in mind, here are the main benefits our system is designed to give you:

- You can make money from the comfort and privacy of your home.

- You can make big money in as little as 10-minutes a day.

- You can get paid a pure passive income... for life!

- You could potentially get paid up to $875 a month – to $5,250 – to as much as $10,500 a month or more, for letting our system help the groups who need to raise money.

This is completely moral – ethical – and even fun! Plus, this gives you the same type of benefits of a very expensive franchise that costs as much as $50,000 to $100,000 or more. This chapter gives you a summary of the main things that make this opportunity so special. I'll cover all of them. Then I'll tell you how to get started.

For starters, there has never been a way to make up to thousands of dollars a month, while also helping so many others at the same time... until now!

AUTOMATIC RECRUITING SYSTEM

THE PROBLEM:

Americans pay some of the highest retail costs for prescription drugs in the world. And even for those who have insurance, the deductibles and co-pays put even necessary drugs out of reach for many families, forcing them to choose between medicine or food. For these families on the fringe, the ability to have one more option that can save them money is a lifesaver.

OUR SOLUTION:

Through a partnership with a major national health technology company, our absolutely free DISCOUNT PRESCRIPTION CARD helps people save money by solving the terrible problem of runaway drug costs. At the time of this writing, our discount prescription cardholders have already saved $179,109,815 off the regular prices of the prescription drugs they need. And those savings increase every single day!

There is a huge and growing need to save up to 87% on all prescription medications – and we have discovered an easy way that YOU can cash-in from the huge demand.

Our core system allows Affiliates to make passive cash by using our easy methods to get our discount drug cards into the hands of the people who desperately need to save money on their prescription medications.

As an affiliate, you can get paid a passive residual income on every prescription filled, when our card was used to get the discount.

Plus, you continue to make money as families go back to the pharmacy for refills and new prescriptions. In fact, once our card is used, it usually stays in the pharmacy's records system, so you can continue to get credit for prescriptions each time they are filled and refilled, month after month.

BUT WAIT... That's only the start of how you make money.

Because Our Easy Passive Income System Lets You Make Even More Money by Tapping into a Massive Source of People Who are Eager to Do All of the Work for You to Get These Discount Cards into the Hands of Hundreds or Thousands of Others...

These people are members of churches or other non-profit groups who need to raise money for all of their various activities.

Our system is designed to let you make money by introducing our program to these non-profit groups. You do one step. We do the rest.

As you've seen, this lets the groups raise the funds they need, while paying you an automatic residual income on all the "work" they do. This has the power to give you complete financial security for life, while doing SO MUCH GOOD for so many others.

We call our program the "Passive Income Fundraising Program."

There are 3 basic components:

1. Helping groups raise money without the headaches and hassles that most fundraisers require...

2. Helping people save money on their prescription medications...

3. And paying YOU passive income!

As you've seen, this is...

The ULTIMATE
SOLUTION

Here's why: All honest and legitimate opportunities solve some kind of major problems for as many people as possible. There is no other way to become financially independent.

Just find millions of people with HUGE PROBLEMS. Then discover or develop a product or service that solves these problems in the BIGGEST WAY. That's it. That's all there is to it. If you can solve a big enough problem for enough people, then you can make a lot of money and enjoy complete and total financial security. This is what you can have when you get involved in this amazing opportunity.

PROBLEM #1:

Millions of people are paying too much for

their prescription drugs. OUR SOLUTION: Our DISCOUNT PRESCRIPTION CARD lets people save up to 87% off on each FDA approved drug at over 54,000 pharmacies nationwide.

PROBLEM #2:

Thousands of groups desperately need to raise money for all of their activities. OUR SOLUTION: Our Passive Income Fundraising Program lets these groups raise the money they need without having to beg friends, family, and neighbors to buy something they don't even want!

PROBLEM #3:

The friends and family of these group members hate the fact that they are constantly being asked to give more money for things they'd never buy otherwise. OUR SOLUTION: The supporters use their free DISCOUNT

PRESCRIPTION CARD to save up to 87% on the prescription drugs they're already taking. This gives them an easy way to help the group raise money, without spending a single dollar. They save money on the medications they need and help the group raise money. Brilliant!

PROBLEM #4:

Many people need a way to make more money, without all of the headaches and hassles. They desperately want to make money with NO long hours, NO large start-up cost and NO personal selling. OUR SOLUTION: As an Affiliate of our Easy Passive Income System, you will use our complete system that lets you make money by helping us introduce our revolutionary program to the groups who desperately need a simple and easy way to raise money. You'll do everything from the comfort and privacy of your own home. This gives you a complete way to get paid a passive monthly income in just minutes a day.

Add it up. You'll see...

EVERYONE WINS!

√   The group wins, because they get an
     easy and automatic way to raise all
     of the money they need for their
     group activities.

√   Their supporters win, because they
     save a lot of money on their
     prescription medications and help the
     group raise money.

√   And YOU WIN, because you can get
     started for a super low fee and then let
     our automated system do everything
     for you. As you'll see, this gives you
     the most powerful way to achieve

complete and total financial security ... and hardly lift a finger.

HOW YOU MAKE MONEY:

You will use our 20-Second System to process mail that introduces our exciting and proven Passive Income Fundraising Program to the groups. Each group is issued a special fundraising code and an initial batch of 5,000 DISCOUNT PRESCRIPTION CARDS they can give away for free. Then every prescription that's filled with this code is credited to you and the group. They receive $1.50 every time each one of their friends and family members use our savings cards, and you earn 35 cents. As you've seen, this small amount can add up to huge profits for you!

It's so simple. It's so brilliant. The groups pass out their DISCOUNT PRESCRIPTION CARDS to their friends and family, along with a special letter that tells them about our unique fundraising program and makes them want to participate. Each time they use the groups card to fill an authorized prescription, the group gets paid, and so do you!

How Much Could You Make?

The amount of commissions you can get is based on the number of your groups that we will be working with [for you], how many savings cards they pass out, and how many people use the cards to fill their prescriptions. Your results will vary based on many factors, so we can't guarantee you'll make any specific sum. But it is possible to make $100,000 a year or more, by using our 20-second system to process mail that introduces our Passive Income Fundraising Program to the non-profit groups and letting them and us do the rest. You can count on us to do all we can to help you make the largest amount of money, because the more you make, the more we make.

So with all that said, let me give you a couple very specific examples that will show you how much money could potentially be generated with our Easy Passive Income System. Remember, these are based on mathematical projections only, but they do a great job of showing you how much money you could potentially make:

EXAMPLE #1:

If you were to use our Easy Passive Income System to sign up only 10 groups who each had 25 members who passed out 10 DISCOUNT PRESCRIPTION CARDS to their friends and family members, and each cardholder fills an average of 1 prescription a month, the groups would get $3,750 a month. That's great news for them! After all, they just raised $3,750 a month and they never had to go through all of the headaches and hassles of most fundraising programs. But it's even better for YOU, because in this example, you would also get your own monthly check for $875.

EXAMPLE #2:

If you had just 10 groups of 150 members each, who passed our free DISCOUNT PRESCRIPTION CARDS to an average of 10 of their friends and family members, and when these people used our savings card to fill an average of 1 prescription a month, you would get paid $5,250 a month. That's $63,000 a year!

EXAMPLE #3:

And if you had just 20 groups of 150 members each, who passed our free DISCOUNT PRESCRIPTION CARDS to 10 of their friends and family members and if these people used our

AUTOMATIC RECRUITING SYSTEM

savings card to fill an average of 1 prescription a month, you'd get paid $10,500 a month in totally passive income!

Those are examples only. I can't promise that you'll get up to $126,000 a year or any specific amount. Your groups could pass out even more DISCOUNT PRESCRIPTION CARDS or have a higher-than-average number of prescriptions filled each month. But as all three of these mathematical examples prove, the potential to get paid as much as $875 to $10,500 a month in passive income or more is here!

But having said all that, you also know:

✔ This lets you make money and rewards you for helping so many other people.

✔ No other home-based business lets you make so much money and do so much good for so many people.

290

✔   This is completely moral – ethical – and even fun! Plus, this gives you all of the same type of benefits of a very expensive franchise that costs as much as $50,000 to $100,000 or more.

✔   And finally: This is totally private. You will never have to talk with anyone (unless you want to). Our company, the DISCOUNT PRESCRIPTION CARD company – and the groups do all of the work for you.

And when you add it all up, you'll realize that, as hard as it may to have believed in the beginning, this really does give you...

The Power to Stay Home Each Day
and Get a Huge Passive Income.

This opportunity lets you get paid on the efforts of many other people. It's the same advantage the most successful people have, and now it's yours for a very low one-time fee.

How it works:

A.   Just fill out the form on the last page of this book and mail or fax it to me. My staff and I will send you complete information about how to become a Representative for our Easy Passive Income System.

B.   Just cover the one-time fee to become a Representative and I will enroll you as an Affiliate for the health technology company who is providing the Prescription Savings Cards. This company is the foundation of our Easy Passive Income System. The low price to become an affiliate for their company will include 5,000 of your own Discount Prescription Cards.

C.   I'll have our health technology partner send your custom-printed Prescription Savings Cards to you. Then I'll rush you my complete Easy Passive Income System. This lets you cash-in with everything you've read about in this book.

THIS IS ONLY FOR YOU.

None of the other Affiliates who are already making money with these Discount Prescription Cards have all of the secrets and turn-key materials you will receive when you become a Representative of our Easy Passive Income System. This could potentially pay you as much as $10,500 a month for only minutes a day. That's potential, not promised income. But – if you've read everything in this book you know – this amazing home business opportunity truly does have the power to pay you huge sums of passive income!

But you must hurry. I can only work with so many people. **The materials you'll be using to introduce the groups to our Fundraising Program all have my personal phone number on them.** My staff and I can only work with so many non-profit groups on a daily basis. Therefore, I'll have to cancel this opportunity whenever I feel we're working with too many groups. If you put this off and fill your position later, you may end up on a waiting list. If that happens, I may never get the chance to do all I can to help you make money.

So let me hear from you at once! An opportunity to get paid as much as thousands of dollars a month for putting in a few minutes a day of easy enjoyable work only comes along once in a lifetime. But you have one here. I hope you take it. Please go to the next page, follow the instructions, and get started today.

CHAPTER NINE

How to Get Started.

I'd like to send you all the details about my Easy Passive Income System today. The complete information package is yours for free. You'll get all the facts. Every "i" is dotted. Every "t" is crossed. You'll look everything over and decide once and for all if this is the perfect way to stay home and make money. If it is, we'll help get you signed up an Affiliate for our revolutionary health technology partner. This company is the foundation of our Easy Passive Income System. They charge a low one-time fee, which we will cover for you. Your Affiliate position will include 5,000 of your own Discount

Prescription Cards. Just fill out the form on the next page and mail or fax it back to my office. I will send you complete information about our Easy Passive Income System. This information package is yours absolutely free. Then, if after looking all this over, this is the perfect way for you to make all the money you want and need, we will enroll you as an Affiliate for the health technology company who is providing the Prescription Savings Cards. And I will make sure they send your 5,000 cards directly to you. Then I will rush you my complete Easy Passive Income System. This lets you cash-in with all of the secrets you've discovered in this book.

"Easy Passive Income System"
FAST-AND-EASY REQUEST FORM

YES! Please tell me more! I read this book and I'm excited! Now I want to know how I can get started. So please rush me the materials that tell me how I can become a representative for the Easy Passive Income System. If accepted into this opportunity, you will help me get set up as an affiliate for the health technology company and do all you can to see to it that I get paid the largest amount of money for doing the most good for so many other people.

RUSH ME THE COMPLETE DETAILS that tell me how I can become a Representative for your Easy Passive Income System! I understand that there's no obligation to get all of these materials.

✔ Provide us your contact information below.

First and Last Name _____

Mailing Address _____

City/State/Zip Code _____

Mobile Phone Number _____

Email Address _____

✔ MAIL or FAX this request form to us right away.

MAIL to: Bethesda Discount Prescriptions • *Old Bethesda Hospital*
103 S. Elm St. • Goessel, KS 67053-0198

FAX to: (620) 367-2261

✔ Or use our ONLINE SUPPORT DESK to provide the info above to request your free Special Report:

www.GetAllTheSecrets.com/epis-info

Invitation Code: ARS

TERMS: For information only. No specific results are guaranteed or implied. Submitting this form grants us permission to communicate with you by mail, fax, phone (live or auto-dial), text message, email or any means necessary to communicate with you.

Still Wondering If This is for Real? Take a Look at What a Few of Our Cardholders Had to Say:

I am senior pastor at My Liberty Church of God and Christ located in Philadelphia, PA in the West Oak Lane section of the city. I pastor about 4,000 people here at the church. The first week after I gave the Card out to my congregation, I got numerous phone calls from the members of the church that they went to the pharmacy, used their Card and had a discount on their prescription. I was amazed. Our church was able to help our members get some discounts where they can be able to manage and budget their money and do other things.

— **Bishop Earnest E. Morris, Sr. (Philadelphia, PA)**

I filled my husband's two prescriptions at our local Hannaford store and I used my card. The first prescription's retail price was $62.99 but I only paid $13.55. The second prescription's retail price was $105.01 but I only paid $14.67 for a 90-day prescription. This was cheaper than the copay on my insurance card through my employer.

— **Sonya MacDonald (South Paris, ME)**

My wife and I befriended a gentleman approximately a year ago who had no health insurance but required medication because of a recent cranial procedure. We purchased his drugs for him at Walgreens at a cost of $297, but this time at renewal we visited our local pharmacy and saved a whopping $240! We recently found out about your organization and are informing several individuals that have no medical coverage. THANK YOU.

Bruce L. (Glassboro, NJ)

My friend is on a catastrophic plan without drug coverage and recently used this card and received a $55 discount without any hassle – super easy and he was very thankful.

— **Allison Nickel (Tacoma, WA)**

My sister-in-law Sonya gave me a card at Wal-Mart here in Columbia, SC. I had just finished shouting at the pharmacy guy telling him, "This is crazy if you think I'm going to pay $68.89 for this prescription!" So my sister-in-law told me to use the card and I did. Wow! Is all I can say. Get this! I paid only $17.64 for my prescription!

— **Pauline Sims (Columbia, SC)**

I'm a diabetic and I have to take diabetic medicine on a regular basis. Through the regular insurance company, I was paying close to $140 for my prescription medicine – four different medications. With the Card, now my medication costs me $50.

— **Nelson Geralds (Pleasantville, NJ)**

We are a prayer group here at Hope Clinic. I plan on giving these to Hope Clinic to give to their patients who are uninsured or under insured. This is why Hope Clinic got started. So people like that could get good healthcare based on their income. They are a non-profit organization. I was blessed with one of your cards that came in the mail. My husband used it first his medicine would have cost him $35 after discount it was just $13.24. I want to share our good fortune with others.

— **Tammy Neville (Lafayette, TN)**

At least one third of our patients are uninsured. They are mostly, really hard working guys that make too much money to qualify for medicaid, but they don't make enough to buy their own insurance. We have patients that take medication that doesn't work very well over a medication that they know works, but can't afford. These cards would be given to our patients that have no insurance, and are in need of some help. This is a great program. I must say, I'm very impressed.

— **Gregory VillaBona, M.D. (Dover, DE)**

My grandson takes the antibiotic Omnicef for ear infections and they have the script filled at Wal-Mart for around $80. She used the card for the refill and it cost her $25.43! When you consider the number of prescriptions filled annually by families (not to mention seniors) the potential economic impact is amazing. We owe it to our families and friends to get the card into their hands!

— **Jerry D. Turney (Scottsdale, AZ)**

I was able to save $69.74 on just one medication. Wow what a blessing.

George Nelson (Mullica Hill, NJ)

www.ingramcontent.com/pod-product-compliance
Lightning Source LLC
Chambersburg PA
CBHW022110210326
41521CB00028B/183